SIMULTANEOUS TRAUMA

THE ROOTS OF DEPRESSION

DISCLAIMER

Before you begin reading, I feel it's important to clarify that the content of this book is deeply personal and drawn entirely from my own life's experiences and personal perspective. The thoughts, reflections, and advice shared throughout these pages are based on how I personally understood and navigated certain moments in my life.

Please keep in mind that this book is not intended to offer medical guidance or replace the expertise of qualified professionals. If you are facing challenges that require medical, psychological, or professional support, I strongly encourage you to seek the help of trained experts.

DEDICATION

I dedicate this book to my mother. You are the greatest example of servitude and know the true meaning of service. I appreciate you for being the most selfless and self-sacrificing person I know. I love you, Mama

TABLE OF CONTENTS

PREFACE

I began writing this book during a pivotal time in my life—while recovering from the depths of severe depression and beginning the difficult process of healing from decades of unresolved trauma. For years, I had silently carried the weight of past wounds, both from my childhood and from experiences that shaped me as an adult.

By the time I reached thirty-nine, I was a single mother of four, caught in the chaos of a painful divorce from my second marriage. In that moment, I felt utterly lost and alone—feeling betrayed by those I trusted and consumed by feelings of victimhood.

I felt shattered into a million pieces, overwhelmed by the question of where to start or how to begin putting the broken fragments of my life back together.

Every day felt like an uphill battle, yet deep inside, I knew I had to keep moving forward. There was a small, flickering part of me that believed healing was possible, even when I couldn't see the way ahead. Writing this book became a lifeline—a way to process my pain and reclaim my voice in the midst of the storm.

After experiencing a powerful panic attack triggered by physical harm from my second ex-husband, I was suddenly struck by overwhelming clarity. That moment of panic forced me to see my reality in a way I never had before.

It was as though I had never truly been present in my own life until that moment—yet everything had always been there, right in front of me. The reality of my situation struck with such force that I felt paralyzed, confused, and unsure how to navigate myself in the aftermath of that horrifying realization.

It felt as though everything that had happened—and everything that was still happening—came crashing down at once, as if it had materialized out of nowhere. I had no choice but to confront it all, facing the truth of my circumstances simultaneously, with no escape.

Fast forward to today—I have healed and recovered from severe CPTSD (Complex Post-Traumatic Stress Disorder), major depression, codependency, generalized anxiety disorder, obsessive-compulsive disorder, narcissistic abuse trauma, as well as deep psychological, emotional, sexual, and severe childhood abuse trauma.

I pulled myself out of that dark and agonizing chapter of my life, where pain, suffering, sadness, and sorrow seemed to be all that existed. No matter how hard I tried to change my circumstances, nothing worked—until a powerful panic attack and a profound moment of awakening shook me to my core, waking me up and changing my life forever.

I wrote this book to share my deeply personal journey of healing from severe trauma and overcoming severe depression. Through this process, I discovered every part of myself—including the pieces I had been searching for my entire life, the parts of me I never knew existed.

In the depths of my depression, I came to understand the true meaning of both light and darkness and the messages they were trying to convey. Some of those messages were horrifying, while others were comforting and reassuring.

My journey through severe depression led me back to my darkest and most agonizing past—one I hadn't realized still lived within me. It resurfaced experiences I had long avoided, things I never wanted to revisit or even remember.

Yet through the process of healing my internal wounds, I discovered the true meaning of courage and experienced what it truly feels like to be courageous—something I never knew I possessed.

When you choose the path to healing, you may rediscover a part of yourself that once seemed long lost—perhaps something you never knew existed or never fully met.

You, yourself, can begin this journey by tracing your footsteps back to where your life began and to where it has led you now. From there, connect each step, filling in the gaps piece by piece, day by day, until the picture becomes clearer and everything starts to make sense.

Today is the day to embark on that uncertain path to healing—a path that may lead you to a place you never thought possible or to a place you never knew existed.

CHAPTER 1

HOW MY PAST LIFE TRAUMAS CAME BACK TO LIFE AND LED TO SEVERE DEPRESSION

In September of 2014, in the midst of a horrifying and very traumatic divorce, I was placed in a situation where I could not react, think, or speak. That experience led to an intense and profound panic attack—one I now refer to as my Awakening Moment because of the powerful impact it had on me.

It was so overwhelming that it felt as though I had been struck by a "Magic Wand," shifting me from a state of sleep and unconsciousness to being fully awake and aware within seconds. From that moment on, my life was never the same.

Two days after being injured by physical abuse, the shock of that incident left me in a state of paralysis. I was unable to react, overcome by confusion and a sense of physical immobility.

The terror, the confusion, and the reality of what was happening felt overwhelmingly real—it was happening to me, in my body. It was as if I was trapped in a horror movie, with myself as the main character. The confusion was horrifying, and the fear was so intense; I could feel the heat in my body rapidly rising.

I remember driving while talking on the phone, shaking and in pain from my injuries, when suddenly a powerful, brilliant "flash" struck my forehead—the front of my head—and everything seemed to pause for a few seconds. I remember looking through my windshield as the world suddenly grew dramatically brighter, and I began to hear silent inner voices I had never heard before.

I started seeing bright colors everywhere I looked, and the horrifying feeling I had moments earlier lifted from my chest, which had felt so full and heavy. For the first time in my life, I felt the subtle yet unmistakably loud beating of my heart.

I quickly put the phone down and drove straight home, wondering what had just happened. This moment marked the beginning of my Self and Life discovery, and my never-ending search for its meaning.

My experience of the panic attack was so powerful and profound that I could not ignore it. From that moment on, everything within me shifted dramatically. I felt lost and overwhelmed, unsure of what to do with myself.

I needed to understand the meaning of that experience, which led me to keep searching for the unexplainable and incomprehensible experiences, that were beyond my mental grasp or capacity to understand.

I was placed in a terrifying situation where panic, combined with an overwhelming buildup of fear and anxiety, led me into a powerful panic attack. It activated my entire consciousness and awakened every part of my being that had been asleep up to that point. That moment marked the beginning of my dark journey into severe depression.

The impact of that intense awakening immediately plunged me into deep depression. It felt as though I was buried alive—mentally and physically paralyzed by overwhelming sadness, exhaustion, and confusion. I suddenly lost interest in everything. I completely checked out.

Everywhere I looked, I saw nothing but shadows and gray, and I felt constantly exhausted and afraid. Even the thought of brushing my teeth or chewing food drained me. I would spend hours thinking about the things I needed to do and often ended up doing nothing at all.

The following morning, I would wake up feeling exactly the same— this cycle went on for years. My state of severe depression deepened to the point where I began hearing voices, while the sensation of physical paralysis grew heavier and heavier. It became so intense that I began to feel everything in every inch of my body.

The feeling grew stronger, as if something were trying to wake me from a very deep sleep. It felt as though I had been heavily drugged, and I was constantly fighting against myself just to get up.

I knew I was in a place I had never been before. I forced myself to function simply to survive each day, feeling as though I was battling something—yet I couldn't identify exactly what I was fighting against.

I also knew it wasn't something medical, because during that period I had seen a doctor twice and was told I was fine—at least physically. I didn't mention my lethargy, confusion, deep sadness, or the heavy, weakened feeling in my body, because I believed I was simply "heartbroken" from my divorce.

As I continued to wonder and reflect on my condition, more experiences began to surface, leading me to keep searching for my own answers. What I was going through was becoming too deep, too dark, and too powerful and heavy to ignore.

The profound feeling of severe depression was so powerful, and because it was such a foreign and unique experience for me, I became intensely aware of it. I wanted to understand what was happening to me.

The darkness of severe depression did not exist only at night. The darkness within me was constant, around the clock. I felt lethargic, as if I were heavily medicated, always on the verge of falling asleep at any moment. The exhaustion was unexplainable, and I felt deeply helpless.

It felt as though I was always on the verge of breaking down in tears for no apparent reason. I initially tried to run from it, forcing myself to go outside or somewhere—anywhere—where I might feel or sense something different. Yet even the thought of doing anything at all sent me back into immediate exhaustion.

Fear, terror, and paranoia became the most dominant emotions, all happening simultaneously. I later learned that this state is medically referred to as **agoraphobia**. I felt intensely anxious and hypervigilant every time I stepped outside my home or attempted to go anywhere.

It was as if anything—or anyone—could be after me, and something terrible could happen at any moment. I had no will and no energy left to fight against those feelings or the heavy physical sensations that came with them.

My severe childhood abuse trauma was coming back to life, and I was re-experiencing the psychological and physical effects of my past as I became more conscious and aware of them.

I lived in a state of severe depression for nearly four years, trying to understand the magnitude of what it meant to be severely depressed. It felt like something had literally placed a black veil over my head, and I was constantly trying to see through it—every hour of every day.

I wondered if I would ever see things clearly, feel "normal" again, and completely emerge from that sense of darkness.

My journey through severe depression was so powerful that my curiosity alone kept me searching for its meaning—eventually leading me to write this book. I wanted to share my story and let you, and others, know that real depression truly exists.

I could not grasp how agonizing depression truly is—until I experienced its physical reality myself. I consciously and courageously faced the battle of severe depression in its deepest and darkest moments, feeling every bit of its effect within me.

It was so deep that I felt it in every cell of my being and heard its echoes in every part of me. I could sense even the roots of my depression—traced back to the severe traumas of my past.

My head felt unbearably heavy, as if it was ready to burst at any moment. My body felt glued to whatever surface I could sit or lie on, overwhelmed by exhaustion around the clock—despite having been physically active all my life.

As I gained more awareness of what I was going through, I kept searching for anything I could find, hoping that somehow, somewhere, I would uncover some answers.

I later self-diagnosed and identified the names of my "disorders", which I knew were caused by many of my unresolved past traumatic and horrifying life experiences and had been keeping me immobilized.

I lived in my one-bedroom apartment with a single dim light on every night, battling depression. It felt like every part of me was being devoured by something only I could sense. I was mentally paralyzed, emotionally numb, and physically weak, yet I forced myself to get up each day to care for my toddler daughter.

Every day I would wake up feeling groggy, then lie on my couch for hours until I could no longer see daylight. I would slowly walk back to bed and wake up the next day feeling the same—terrified, confused, anxious, hypervigilant, and utterly exhausted despite sleeping ten to fourteen hours the night before. This was my life for four years, around the clock.

With each passing day, every feeling, thought, physical movement, and sensation became more noticeable as my awareness grew. Yet I was mentally paralyzed, unable to respond to anything. I couldn't understand why I suddenly felt like I was living in a completely different world.

I was fighting my condition every second of every day, constantly trying to identify what I was going through. It felt unreal, far removed from my usual daily life.

It all started in that moment of a powerful flash, when I suddenly became completely awake—able to sense and hear every subtle detail inside and outside of my being. Yet there were still not enough words to describe it or fully articulate the experience.

As I continued to fight against my depression, it only seemed to pull me deeper. It felt as though there was something more to understand, something connected beneath the surface of my experience. That curiosity led me to discover that:

> The multiple symptoms of my depression were only the dead branches of a thirty-nine-year-old tree. The roots remained intact, fully alive and functioning as my active past and unconscious traumas.

The longer I stayed severely depressed, the more I began to recognize the reasons behind it. Glimpses of vivid memories from my past started to clear the way, allowing me to see and understand my journey through depression.

This realization and awareness of my past marked the beginning of my healing journey. I began to recognize the divide between being asleep and becoming more conscious and aware of what I was truly experiencing.

As I become more aware, I learned to consciously choose between love and pain whenever I was triggered, and in whatever experience was presented to me. I came to understand that both are always present, and that I had the power to choose which one to move toward.

Love and Pain are both essential to feel during healing and to experience in order for us to be fully alive. They help us remain conscious and aware, so we can make clearer, wiser choices and decisions.

Severe depression awakened my whole being in the most profound and excruciating way. The experiences were so unique, so deep, and so unfamiliar that I felt compelled to understand their meaning. Which eventually led me to heal every part of my wounded being.

I healed the psychological and emotional traumas I had accumulated and endured throughout my life, which were the roots of my severe depression. In doing so, I was able to pull myself out of that state.

The brutal impact of severe depression activated every part of myself, forcing me to become wide awake and re-experienced my past. It made me feel the full spectrum of human emotion and experience. Having lived through it all, I suddenly felt connected to everything in life.

The profound and powerful effects of severe depression gave me new meaning and new ways to live and experience life. It allowed me to see reality more fully and recognize the multidimensional nature of my existence.

Even my own mortality no longer frightens me—suddenly, I am at peace with the idea of dying. It no longer matters when I leave this Earth, because I have come to accept this reality as a certain fact of life.

In fact, understanding and accepting my mortality has taught me to live each day as if it could be my last. Not in a careless or reckless way, but by living as fully and as well as I can, and by connecting with others as kindly and lovingly as possible.

When I began healing myself, every part of me—and everything in my life—started to change drastically, faster than I was prepared for.

My journey into severe depression came out of nowhere and hit me with such force that I did not know how to respond to the experience, because I did not yet understand what I was going through.

I began to recognize that I was living in a very strange, unfamiliar, and dark place—not tied to any particular location or time of day. The darkness and the unfamiliar feeling of severe depression followed me around the clock, day and night. That was when I realized I had entered a place I had never been before.

Severe depression was an agonizing experience, but its unfamiliar intensity also made me deeply curious about what was truly happening to me.

After four years of battling severe depression and eventually finding my own way out of that state, I now understand that depression is a natural human condition and a part of the human experience.

It is natural, yet profoundly powerful, and unique to each individual who has experienced or is currently experiencing it.

I now think of this human condition as the "Sleeping Demon"—something most of us will encounter and struggle with at some point in our lives, often rooted in unresolved trauma and past experiences.

> Depression pushed every part of my being to its limits
> and forced me to confront and conquer my own internal
> battle.

I was aware and courageous enough to sit with the agony during the darkest moments of that journey. I also understood that I was the only person who could pull myself out of that state—by understanding where it came from and healing its roots, which were my unresolved past traumas.

When I realized that I was not alone on this journey called the "Roller Coaster of Life," I chose the higher road—the unknown path—and took full responsibility for myself, accepting everything that had happened to me.

Regardless of whose fault it was, I forgave myself for allowing myself to suffer for so long. Then life began to shift in the direction I had always wished and hoped it would go.

At thirty-nine, I was completely dependent on others for both my internal and external needs because I had become a product of my very broken upbringing, recreating my life from that wounded place. I was deeply hurt, emotionally shattered, and felt completely empty—crippled, helpless, and powerless.

But that person was me—and here I am now, sharing my life story with you, because I know I am not alone. I am here to tell you that I am living proof of how miraculous life can be when you choose the path of healing and commit to changing yourself for the better, regardless of your past.

I am living proof that when you believe in the impossible, everything becomes possible. But if you believe you are a victim of what has happened—or what is happening—in your life, you will remain bound to the energy of the past and trapped in pain and suffering.

My life, from the day I was conceived, felt like a never-ending chain of traumatic and horrifying events. At times, it seemed as though I had crossed countless dangerous paths simply to stay alive.

When I finally faced the realities of both my past and present, it felt as if I had no memory of where I had been throughout my life or how I had arrived at this moment. Yet, in the depths of my depression, I found the answers I had been searching for.

I was a lost and wounded person for the first thirty-nine years of my life, with little conscious awareness of my past choices and the mistakes shaped by decades of life's traumas.

When we are in pain, we tend to see only the pain within us and around us, responding to everything from that place.

Our past and present life experiences—the good, the bad, and the ugly—hold equal value as lessons we can learn from and apply in our daily lives. The wisdom we gain and the lessons we extract from these experiences can become a solid foundation for a better, happier life—once we choose to accept them, heal from them, and come to terms with them.

Like most people—and this could be you—I was once an out-of-control person with no life direction, simply living a life dictated, directed, and shaped by others. I was living in the energy of my past, and everything I did was driven by the traumas of my early life.

I grew up having to take care of myself as if I had been left alone in the middle of a jungle from birth. I learned to survive on my own in a very dysfunctional, brutal, and hostile home environment, shaped by my father's severe alcohol addiction and abusive behavior, and my mother's extreme co-dependency.

I want to share my life's story with the hope that, somehow, somewhere out there, whoever is reading this might feel inspired to do the same.

Once we become adults, we are fully responsible for ourselves—our lives, our happiness and well-being, and our survival—regardless of our past or how our parents or caregivers raised us.

When you reach the point where your parents or caregivers are no longer responsible for your personal choices and decisions, you have the power to take control of your life and make better choices for yourself.

It begins with understanding yourself, your past conditioning, and regaining your identity; recognizing your abilities and your capacity; and taking the steps to create the life you truly want for yourself now.

CHAPTER 2

UNDERSTANDING MY CHILD ABUSE, RAPE, AND SEXUAL ABUSE TRAUMAS

I grew up in a very hostile, toxic, horrifying, and very dysfunctional home, shaped by my father's severe alcohol addiction and his destructive, abusive, and violent behavior.

There wasn't a single day that I saw my father sober. Being the oldest of three children, I became the favorite target of his cruelty. My mother was completely helpless and powerless, trapped in her own co-dependency, unable to protect me.

If she tried, she would have been the one to suffer. All she could do was watch as I was tortured and physically beaten by my father—nearly every day.

As I began my healing process and revisited my childhood memories, a vivid scene came to life:

I saw my mother standing in a corner of our house, watching me as my father beat me. I cannot imagine being in her position—watching your own child suffer and feeling powerless to do anything to protect them.

I also remember another scene very vividly, even to this day.

One night, my father came home crawling drunk while we were all asleep. He woke us and forced us to line up, holding a gun, making us choose between him and my mother. I was the only one who chose to be with him—out of sheer terror, fearing what he might do to me if I didn't.

There was not a single day when I felt safe in my own home or around the people who were supposed to comfort and protect me. Every night when I went to bed, I felt as though my father was always ready to attack me.

Because of this constant fear, I came to understand what it might feel like to be a soldier in a war zone, standing in the middle of a battlefield.

I lived as if I were constantly being hunted, believing that at any moment I could be hurt or killed. There were knives swinging, guns pointed at us, belts, hands, and fists striking us—myself, my mother, and my brother. And I was almost always the first and primary target of my father's physical, verbal, and emotional abuse and brutality.

Then the next day, our lives would return to "normal," as if nothing terrible had happened the day before. Living amid daily hostility, violence, and destruction had become my normal life. This was the environment I grew up in for the first thirteen years of my life.

After years of recalling and reflecting on my childhood experiences—driven by a deep longing to resolve my unresolved past and confusion—one day, I finally came to understand that:

> I was born and raised by two very young, broken, and wounded parents. One was an abusive alcohol addict, and the other was a helpless, co-dependent parent trying to raise a family. They were doing the best they knew how to raise children and build a family—but unfortunately, their "best" often caused the worst harm, and they simply did not know any better.

I carried the trauma from that home environment for thirty-nine years, completely unaware of how those experiences had shaped and controlled the dynamics of my life—until I became consciously aware of my past.

I lived in a state of severe depression and developed multiple conditions, including Complex Post-Traumatic Stress Disorder (CPTSD), Generalized Anxiety Disorder, Agoraphobia, Nervous Habits, Fibromyalgia (sharp nerve pain that could strike anywhere in my body at any time), Obsessive-Compulsive Disorder (OCD), and Perfectionism—where I would repeat tasks over and over to the point of complete mental distortion.

I lived my life unconsciously terrified of almost everything, unable to control my reactions. My triggers were so severe that any person, situation, or event could provoke an uncontrollable response, and I had no idea why.

I learned to silence my reactions early on because expressing myself wasn't allowed in my childhood. What began as a survival strategy eventually became a habit—one that followed me into adulthood and shaped how I responded in relationships.

I developed the traits and behaviors of both my parents combined. I became emotionally shut down and frozen, unconsciously hurting myself and others simply through the way I coped and tried to protect myself.

> For the first thirteen years of my life, I lived in survival mode, fighting for my life every hour of every day because of my own father. Through this experience, I came to understand what it must feel like to be a soldier on a battlefield—hiding in every corner I could fit into—so the enemy could not see me, because the moment I was seen, I would be hurt or tortured.

My father and the home environment he created became my real-life nightly horrors and nightmares. I became a restless person, always on alert, ready to run or hide.

The traumatic impact of that brutal environment later followed me into my journey with severe depression, continuing to haunt me long afterward.

> I remember lying in bed at night as a child, always waiting and anticipating being called by my father. The moment I heard his voice; my body would begin to shake uncontrollably.

The psychological and emotional trauma of my past crippled me internally and drained the sense of safety from my entire being. I spent my life searching for people, places, and environments where I could feel protected and secure.

Yet I continued to attract—and repeatedly end up in—the same kinds of people, places, and environments: abusive people, harsh surroundings, and destructive situations. Pain, violence, hostility, and chaos had become familiar to me, and familiarity had come to feel like comfort.

I eventually became aware of my traumas and recognized that they were the driving forces behind my choices, behaviors, and the types of people I kept attracting into my life.

When I began the healing process and started revisiting my childhood, those memories came flooding back and began to haunt me again. As I recalled these experiences, I felt physically nauseous, as if I might throw up, because I was bringing the darkest and most horrifying memories to the surface.

> I remember recalling moments when my father came
> home extremely drunk—just hearing his voice in my
> memory made my body shake. Suddenly, intense physical
> sensations rushed through me, as if someone or some-
> thing were standing behind me while I relived those
> events.

The terror I had felt as a child resurfaced with overwhelming force, returning in seconds the very first time it happened.

The more I recalled these events, the fewer emotional and physical reactions surfaced. After years of healing, reflection, and revisiting my painful past, one day, everything became just memories.

The emotional trauma that had been attached to those experiences lifted from my body and diminished completely—leaving only memories to remember.

Understanding the source of my pain and suffering, I realized that my father was a very broken and wounded young man. Drowning himself in alcohol was his way of coping, numbing his own pain.

His cowardly behavior, which hurt his family, gave him a false sense of power, comfort, and strength to compensate for the suffering he carried inside.

My father was no different from anyone else struggling under the weight of a broken upbringing. Having no one to talk to when he needed to be heard, he turned to alcohol and sought power as a local leader—chasing external recognition to fill the void he felt internally.

His pursuit never ended because he never took the time—or had the courage—to face the internal struggles that drove him like a madman. He passed away at the age of fifty-nine, while I was still battling severe depression.

Knowing my own pain and suffering, and understanding where it all came from, I realized that even if I had a chance to confront my father, revisiting the past would have been irrelevant. There was nothing he could tell me that I did not already know and understand.

I had already found all the answers we both needed to be free—by understanding the root causes of my own pain and suffering, and the roots of his behavior.

MY RAPE AND SEXUAL ABUSE TRAUMA: Beyond growing up in a very hostile and violent home, we were also part of a cult-like religious practice. I was highly isolated from any male who was not a family member—because, as brutal as my father was, he was also extremely protective and controlling.

The moment I gathered enough courage to leave; I walked out of the house at thirteen with the intention of never coming back.

When I got to the small town where I grew up and was walking along the side of the street, a man who was as old as, or older than my father, approached me and asked if I was alone. The next thing I knew, he was on top of me, and the monster had raped me.

I lost my virginity in a rape at thirteen to a complete stranger on the side of the street. It happened so fast that by the time I began to feel sensation in my body, the monster had already taken off and disappeared from my sight. It was dark, and he did what he did so quickly that I never even saw his face or what he looked like.

Then came the next child rapist within a few hours while I was wandering around the same area. Another monster abducted me and took me away from where they found me. He used and abused me sexually for a few weeks, then took me to a prostitution place run by a woman he knew.

Luckily, before anything worse happened to me, a much older gentleman who recognized my vulnerability saved me. Ironically, a few weeks later, I was informed that my abductor and second rapist was stabbed to death and had died. I felt absolutely nothing while listening to the person delivering the news.

I developed a very strong ability to suppress physical and emotional pain and mastered how to remain quiet. I learned to internalize pain every time my father was hurting me. I was never allowed to cry or react, even when I was severely hurting.

This ability is what saved me from the men who raped and abused me. I developed the strong ability to inhale and internalize pain without blinking an eye, as my way to cope and protect myself.

From the experienced of being raped and sexually abused by older men who were very old — some as old as my grandfather — I developed a severe dependency on men for both my internal and external needs. I found myself drawn to men, as if they could instantly fill the emptiness my father had never been able to fill.

After years of deliberate healing, and when I finally connected the dots, I no longer saw any of those men as bad people. Even with my agonizing experiences with my father and the men who raped me.

I now see each of them as wounded and desperate people — and I happened to be the one who was available to them at that time.

As powerless and vulnerable young girl, I was an easy prey for the men who raped me and a vent for my father's pain and internal suffering. Even with my father's very painful ways of showing love, I never once doubted that he loved me — and I hold this truth to this day.

When I left home, I attracted hurtful and abusive men because I was just one of them: a very wounded and very vulnerable young girl who was looking for a father.

Those men gave me that comfort, even if that comfort came from sexually submitting to them and obeying them — because that was where I felt safe. I said yes to everything, even when I was hurting.

As I became a young woman, I developed a need to please every man I met—until I became conscious and aware of this pattern. I then went back to learning and understanding my own behavior and the trauma behind it.

Each time I recognized this repetitive behavior, I brought the underlying trauma and the memory connected to it to the surface by revisiting my childhood experiences. When I found myself in similar situations again, I was able to stop them from happening and saved myself from continuing to get hurt.

I spent thirty-nine years of my life seeking attention from men—hoping and longing to be loved and protected, and wishing they would never leave me. This longing came from the empty space within me, created by constant rejection, abandonment, feeling unloved, and feeling deeply unsafe around my father.

After years of conscious healing, those once-familiar traumas began to feel new and unfamiliar. Every man I met became a stranger to me, because I no longer resonated with them. That was when I knew I was healing from those wounds.

Over time, as I studied and came to understand the traits of each person who raped and sexually abused me, I initially felt enraged when I fully grasped the age gap between I and my rapists.

But healing through understanding brought clarity: had they been in a healthy state of mind—mentally stable or internally well—they would have had the conscience to stop themselves, knowing how young I was in comparison.

Yes, there are people who walk around looking to hurt others, and their targets are often the powerless and vulnerable—like I was. But through years of healing and understanding my own wounds and brokenness, I came to see that we were drawn to one another because we were all internally disturbed, lost, empty, hurt, and broken.

I happened to be around them when I was a very vulnerable, helpless, innocent, naïve, and powerless young girl—an "easy prey."

My father was a clear example of this. I watched him as I grew up, and his behavior never changed. When I finally reached my own level of maturity, my father seemed to become more and more like a child—behaving unconsciously and never growing up or maturing.

Having to witness this reality, it was very hard for me to turn against my father and blame him for what he did and for what happened to me. I watched my father slowly destroy himself through alcohol addiction, largely unconsciously.

As I became more awake and aware of what was happening within me and around me, and as I observed people's harmful behaviors, I came to see that most adults are often like young children, acting and behaving unconsciously.

This realization helped me understand that my abusers were among those people—unaware of what they were doing or unable to see the future consequences of their choices, because they were driven by their own pain or by the need to fill their internal voids to survive.

I know now that my rapists and sexual abusers were like many people who make choices driven by their own pain. They were unconsciously hurting and suffering. And if pain is all you know, pain is all you have to give.

I healed by understanding where all of our wounds came from—mine, my two rapists', and my abusers'. Through healing by understanding, forgiveness arose naturally.

That same understanding transformed pain into love and compassion—not only for myself, but also for them—because I now see and understand the origins of all our wounds.

CHAPTER 3

UNDERSTANDING MY DESTRUCTIVE AND ABUSIVE RELATIONSHIPS

Both of my marriages were continuations of my childhood experiences and trauma. I married two men who embodied traits and personalities similar to a combination of my father and brother.

The dynamics of both marriages reflected the patterns I witnessed growing up — the relationships I observed, absorbed, and internalized.

In many ways, I recreated my parents' marriage through my own two marriages. The familiarity of those dynamics is why I stayed for so long; they felt normal to me because they were all I had ever known.

As I became more aware of what was truly happening in my marriages, I began to recognize that my life after leaving home at thirteen was simply a continuation of the life I had grown up with — one that felt strangely comfortable, even though it was destructive and painful. I did not know another way to live, because pain and destruction was all I had ever known.

MY FIRST MARRIAGE

In this marriage, the dynamic closely mirrored the relationship between my father and I growing up, because my ex-husband was only one year younger than my father. Our relationship felt more like that of a father and daughter than that of equal partners or husband and wife.

With him, I recognized the same familiar dominant traits I had seen in my father — in the way he demanded things be done and in the way he treated me. Everything had to be perfect and meticulously controlled.

My ex-husband's perfectionism, controlling nature, and behavior toward me were almost identical to how my father had treated me.

The reason I stayed in this marriage for a decade was not because I was happy, but because it felt familiar. It mirrored the life I had grown up with.

> I remember making breakfast, where even cooking an egg had to be done perfectly — so precisely that I felt I could not blink without making a mistake. And when I stepped out of the shower, I was followed and told to pick up a single strand of hair from the floor.

Just like a father who orders a daughter around to clean up after herself, I recognized that, as a wife, I was trapped in the same familiar dynamic — being controlled and treated like a small child.

After years of re-experiencing that familiar trauma, memories of my childhood with my father resurfaced. I began to hear my father's voice in my ex-husband's words and to see my father's behavior reflected in his actions.

After nearly a decade of being scrutinized and controlled, I finally realized that I had married a man who was just like my father — and that I was responding to him in the same way I had responded to my father growing up.

MY SECOND MARRIAGE

In this marriage, I became my mother — married and severely codependent with someone who had an addictive and abusive personality. This person was also a pathological covert narcissist.

He embodied the traits and personalities of both my father and my brother combined, which were reflected in his behavior and character. My ex-husband's destructive behavior closely resembled my father's, and I found myself responding to him in the same way my mother had responded to my father.

His destructive and highly abusive behavior often triggered memories of how my father treated my mother. After years of psychological, verbal, and emotional abuse — along with repeated cycles of destruction, multiple breakups, and separations — I began to recognize the pattern.

The memories of my parents' very destructive marriage
resurfaced and came back to life.

I became attached to this person because his personality and behavior triggered deep memories of my parents' relationship, which kept me tied to the relationship. Eventually, I recognized that I was literally reliving the hostility and brutality of my parents' marriage in my own life.

The emotional highs and lows — along with the psychological and emotional abuse — felt so familiar that I continued to tolerate them. Over time, I began to see myself acting and responding just like my mother.

> The traumatic memories of my parents' marriage were reactivated by my ex-husband's similar behavior and by the nearly identical home environment we had created together.

UNDERSTANDING MY NARCISSISTIC ABUSE TRAUMA

In this relationship dynamic, the trauma I carried from being constantly gaslighted by my brother and repeatedly abandoned, discarded, and neglected by my parents was reactivated by my ex-husband's similar behavior. Being discarded and constantly rejected mirrored exactly how I had often felt growing up.

After years of repeated rejection and emotional abandonment by my ex-husband, my past began to resurface. His familiar patterns of behavior activated the deepest wounds in me — the longing for love, safety, and validation that I had carried since childhood.

During the early stage of our relationship, his love-bombing tactics felt like everything I had been searching for my entire life — as if the universe had finally granted me what I had always wanted.

The intense attention, praise, and illusion of unconditional love were things I had never experienced growing up, and the narcissist appeared to give me all of it.

I was completely engulfed by this person's love-bombing, even though it felt too good to be true — and it was. About a year into our relationship, his behavior toward me began to rapidly change and became increasingly complicated and destructive. This shift led to nearly a decade of chaos and multiple forms of abuse.

But why did I stay? Why did I allow and tolerate the abuse and participate in the destruction? At the time, I could not see it clearly — because my actions were driven by unresolved trauma and a deep emotional emptiness that longed to be filled and comforted.

He initially activated my childhood wounds of abandonment, gaslighting, neglect, manipulation, and the constant longing for my parents' attention. At first, he seemed to fill the voids within me, and I wanted to stay in that illusion of connection and relief.

As the relationship continued, the abuse grew worse, yet everything still felt disturbingly familiar. My ex-husband constantly triggered my childhood fears of rejection and abandonment, especially during important occasions and through repeated threats of divorce.

After years of enduring and absorbing what had become a painfully familiar pattern of psychological, emotional, and verbal abuse, one day the physical violence finally occurred — and only then did I fully wake up to the realization that I had been reliving the dynamics of my childhood and the way I was raised.

In that moment, I saw reflections of my younger self, my brother, my mother, and my father playing out within this relationship. The same patterns, behaviors, and emotional roles resurfaced — appearing in flashes of familiar memories and past family dynamics, triggered by both my ex-husband's behavior and my own responses within the marriage.

My narcissistic abuse trauma was the most excruciating and had the deepest impact on my psyche because of how profoundly this person's behavior excavated my deepest wounds.

The psychological trauma and lingering effects of narcissistic abuse tend to persist for a long time, largely because narcissists target unhealed wounds and unresolved trauma.

Through gaslighting, deception, and intense manipulation, it often feels as though they know exactly where to "dig" — precisely identifying the vulnerabilities of the person they are trying to pull in.

Their distorted way of thinking twists reality, leaving you disoriented and spinning as your deepest wounds are repeatedly triggered in the very places that most need healing.

I came to recognize that pathological narcissists often prey on highly vulnerable individuals, and I witnessed and experienced this firsthand during and after my relationship with one. I eventually realized that I had been gaslighted and manipulated to the point of near psychological collapse.

The imprint of narcissistic abuse remains with me to this day, regardless of how much I understand or how aware I have become of my trauma and the nature of narcissism.

The rape trauma, by comparison, had less impact because it was not nearly as painful, complex, or confusing as the trauma of narcissistic abuse.

Pathological narcissists engage in extremely damaging psychological games through gaslighting, causing you to question your own sanity, beliefs, and sense of self on every possible level.

Over time, you can lose the ability to trust your own perceptions or even recognize what is being done to you. I had to painfully rewire my thinking and reconnect my sense of reality in order to regain my mental stability.

Being in a relationship with a pathological narcissist is very intense and very complicated on every level. One day they claim to love you completely, and the next day you mean nothing to them.

They possess a powerful ability to manipulate and reshape those who are vulnerable, confused, deeply wounded, unaware, or lacking self-awareness — because they have learned how to maneuver around people through calculated manipulation.

These types of people, or those with narcissistic personality traits, have a unique ability to manipulate, engulf, twist, or undermine anyone's sanity and sense of self almost instantly. The higher they are on the narcissistic spectrum, the more extreme and damaging their behavior becomes.

The severity of narcissistic abuse trauma depends on how long you were involved with the narcissist and how unaware or unconscious you were of what they were doing — both to you and to themselves.

Pathological narcissists, or those with NPD, are ultimately broken, wounded, and traumatized individuals, much like anyone else who has experienced pain.

According to **Dr. Ramani Durvasula**, an expert on narcissism: most narcissists are products of their own upbringing.

As I was healing from this trauma and still having to remain in contact with this person due to our shared parenting obligations, I saw everything with my eyes wide open. I witnessed, fully aware, how they intentionally hurt others with contempt and a disturbing sense of satisfaction.

From my experience, knowledge, and understanding of pathological narcissists (or NPDs), I have learned that they cope with their own pain by hurting others.

Their lack of empathy, combined with a strong sense of entitlement, makes them feel completely justified in their actions — believing that the other person "deserves" it.

NO EMPATHY is the very nature of narcissists, which can be extremely difficult to accept or understand if you are not aware of it or don't have enough knowledge about narcissism.

As I healed from my narcissistic abuse trauma, I closely observed four narcissistic men. From my experience and understanding of narcissists (or NPDs), I realized that yes, they are deeply hurtful people who intentionally harm others with complete satisfaction, driven by their lack of empathy and inability to feel for others.

This is why it is so difficult for survivors of narcissistic abuse to forgive them. You may ask: How can you forgive someone who takes pleasure in hurting others and believes they are completely justified in doing so?

They can place a person into instant paralysis the moment that person realizes they have been twisted and manipulated to the point of mental distortion. Becoming involved with narcissistic individuals often becomes a losing battle.

Between the put-downs, gaslighting, heavy manipulation, love bombing, betrayal, deception, sexual exploitation, hot-and-cold treatment, and eventual discard — the cycle is relentless.

So, do narcissists know what they are doing? After closely observing four pathological narcissists (or individuals with NPD) throughout my healing journey, my answer is YES — they are aware of their actions.

However, they often lack the ability to behave differently because they don't know another way. They don't yet have the internal emotional resources to change, unless and until they begin healing the root causes of their narcissistic behavior.

Their habits and behaviors are driven by their own internal needs to survive — needs that are often referred to as **"narcissistic supply."** This can include gaslighting, manipulation, sexual exploitation, deception, betrayal, and various addictions.

Another truth about pathological narcissists is that they don't necessarily want to hurt anyone — at least not consciously. When they realize the harm they have caused, they may feel guilty about their actions.

What truly causes pain is their lack of empathy and inability to emotionally connect with others. They simply cannot feel for or relate to anyone in a meaningful way.

Coupled with their arrogance and strong sense of entitlement — both core narcissistic traits — they believe they can act however they want and treat others however they choose.

I remember after I got injured and finally had a face-to-face conversation with this person about what he had done. An empathetic person would immediately apologize sincerely, knowing they had caused harm — but not a narcissist.

Narcissists see it as your fault because they are incapable of putting themselves in someone else's pain due to their lack of empathy. They know they are hurting you, and often they do it intentionally, deriving satisfaction as their way to cope.

Because they lack empathy, they don't care about the harm they cause. They simply can't and don't know how to put themselves in another person's position or understand the experience of being emotionally hurt.

This is the very nature of pathological narcissists — and the higher they are on the spectrum, the less empathetic and more "cold-hearted" they become.

The good, the bad, and the ugly traits of pathological narcissists became even clearer to me as I was writing this book. Out of nowhere, I attracted another one. Why? Familiarity. But this time, I immediately recognized who I was dealing with.

I decided to experiment by getting involved with this person in a non-committed relationship, staying long enough to study them and look for answers — to understand them better. They absolutely could never relate to me on an emotional level.

They don't understand how you feel, no matter how many ways you try to explain your emotions or express yourself on deeply personal subjects. I remember bringing up my children in a conversation and receiving the same reaction — no emotion at all.

I realized that they avoid conversations involving deep or heavy emotions and anything beyond surface-level topics, simply because they cannot relate to them.

I also recognized consistent patterns in how they communicate and behave — the passive-aggressive actions, the indirect cruelty, and the deliberate use of hurtful words to cause emotional pain.

They are highly skilled at twisting reality through gaslighting and manipulation — like looking at a blue sky and trying to convince you it is red, and if you disagree, making you question your own sanity.

Everything they do is conditional. They are restless individuals with fragile egos and very low self-esteem. They are especially sensitive to criticism, particularly regarding their physical appearance or personal achievements, and can react very easily when they feel threatened.

I also noticed that their generosity was rarely genuine. Their "generosity" often comes with an instant reward — feeding their narcissistic needs or their hunger for praise and adoration. If they don't receive the acknowledgment they expect, their conditional generosity stops immediately.

They would parade you around and take you to fancy places, not necessarily because they could afford it, but to show you off to the world and feel grandiose. This is also why pathological narcissists are often drawn to attractive partners — it enhances their image and sense of superiority.

My narcissistic abuse trauma was, in a way, healed by the narcissist himself — simply by remaining present during my healing process.

As I worked on myself, I began to see him from completely different perspectives, through new angles and insights.

That experience, along with interactions with another narcissist, helped me understand why they behave the way they do and why they are the way they are.

At one point, I even reasoned with myself that maybe I could get involved with a narcissist again, now armed with the knowledge I had gained. But I knew they are not the type of people who can truly relate to anyone emotionally because of their cold-blooded nature and lack of empathy.

Most narcissists cannot sustain a healthy relationship for long because they lack the ability to connect with anyone on a deep emotional level.

I have tried and tested every possibility of having a "healthy" relationship with narcissistic people — whether in intimate relationships, with family members, or with friends — time and time again. Eventually, I completely lost hope.

So, walk away, for your own sake and sanity. Unless you have experienced abuse by a narcissist, have sufficient knowledge of their nature, or are emotionally strong enough to recognize their unconscious behaviors, you will never fully know when you are being heavily manipulated, gaslighted, or drawn into their world.

> The very nature of pathological narcissists is their **lack of empathy**, and it is their inability to feel for others that makes them mean, hurtful, and heartless individuals. They can act kind and speak words of love and compassion, but they don't truly feel them. This is why

they can shift almost instantly from being loving to being mean and hurtful.

I spent a great deal of time studying these people as I healed from my narcissistic abuse trauma. Learning about and understanding the nature of pathological narcissists (or NPDs) is what ultimately allowed me to rise above my narcissistic abuse trauma.

So, if or when you become involved with someone who seems cold, abusive, and unempathetic, they may be a narcissist.

Knowing what I know now about narcissists, destructive, and abusive people—and understanding how I attracted them — apologies or explanations may feel great, but they are ultimately irrelevant. Forgiveness becomes automatic.

Because now I understand that:

Hurt people hurt people

Stupid people do stupid things

Desperate people do desperate things

Unstable people do dangerous things

Not because they want to, but because of how they are and where they are psychologically. And we all carry these tendencies to some degree, depending on where we are in our personal journey.

UNDERSTANDING THE DYNAMIC OF ABUSIVE RELATIONSHIPS

As part of my healing process, while recalling past life events, I had very profound experiences about the stages of healing and how revisiting trauma can sometimes be even more painful and excruciating than the original events themselves.

It can feel more painful than the actual event because, when you become fully conscious and awake, you absorb and feel everything much more intensely. This is in contrast, to when you were only partially aware and unable to fully experience the impact of the event at the time.

For much of my adult life, I attracted people very similar to those I was around growing up — destructive, abusive, wounded, and hurt individuals — because these were the types of people I was familiar with and felt comfortable being around.

Only when I began to see the reality of my current life — the kinds of people and relationships I had with friends, romantic partners, and family members — did I realize that I was still living in the same environment and surrounding myself with the same types of people I grew up with.

Having witnessed and experienced my parents' relationship dynamic, including the hostility between them, and seeing how I had recreated that same life for myself, I wanted to understand why.

So, I carefully observed both my own behavior and that of my second ex-husband, examining how events unfolded and why abuse or hostility arises in any type of relationship. I wanted to understand why people "stay" in abusive, destructive, and hurtful situations despite the pain.

This is what I recognized from my parents' marriage and observed in my own:

In any destructive or abusive relationship — regardless
of the personalities or personality disorders involved —
there are always two people in the dynamic. One may take
the role of the "abused" and the other the "abuser," but
both are always participating and co-creating the dynamics of the relationship, whether it is healthy or unhealthy.

There is no singular victim — and if there is, there are two. There is no
singular abuser — and if there is, there are two. Why? no abuser can
abuse or hurt anyone if there are no victims present. Period. There is
no war if there are no enemies. Period.

Both individuals are simultaneously abusing and victimizing one another by co-creating the dynamic, whether they are fully aware of their
participation or not. A relationship is always a two-way street.

The reason one person often plays the victim is that they feel more
vulnerable and less powerful. The person perceived as the abuser is
usually the one who feels superior, more powerful, and in control —
which gives them the ability to hurt or dominate the other. Meanwhile,
the other person allows, tolerates, or participates in the abuse.

Unless you are physically restrained or locked in and truly powerless to
make a choice, "staying" in an abusive relationship is, in itself, a form
of participation.

My mother and I could have left our marriages, but we stayed — we
allowed, we participated, and we tolerated.

I recognize that most people who are involved in abusive or destructive
relationships are wounded or broken in some way. Otherwise, they
would not be caught in such dynamics.

Both individuals are responding or reacting from their own pain, creating an environment that may be destructive or hurtful — yet both derive some form of relief or comfort as a way to cope.

Often, the familiar patterns of destruction they experienced growing up, or the familiar behaviors they adopt, fill the voids within them.

These voids may reflect the familiar feeling of being hurt, or the familiar sense of power and superiority gained from hurting others. Pain and destruction have become their "normal."

As a result, they tolerate living in abusive or destructive situations and continue to co-create the only life they know — until they become aware of the root causes of their destructive behaviors.

We are treated by others to the degree that we accept, participate in, and allow them to treat us. Most abuse doesn't happen overnight. We don't simply wake up one morning to find our entire lives changed by a single unwanted event or circumstance.

Aside from sudden, obvious life incidents or emergencies, the most impactful events in life usually occur incrementally, in small stages. Hints, signs, nudges, aches and pains, warnings, and signals are everywhere — and we sense them.

Yet, we are often lost, hurt, or broken, or we simply don't pay attention because we are seeking something else to comfort our pain or fill the emptiness within us. Many abusive relationships develop gradually in small stages, progressing over time to the point of complete destruction.

We often ignore the signs because we are blinded by what is happening inside of us. Our ability to see clearly is clouded by our own suffering, caused by unconscious and unresolved psychological and emotional trauma.

After years of abuse in my second marriage, one day the unforgivable act occurred. The shocking impact of that incident hit me all at once, as if the years of accumulated events had struck like a tsunami.

By then, the damage was done, and the trauma was already deeply imprinted in me, because living in a destructive relationship and enduring abuse had become my "normal" life.

It was only on the day I was physically injured that I realized this major incident was the result of years of smaller ones — all of which I had been ignoring, accepting, participating in, and allowing. The abuse had started with offensive name-calling and gradually escalated to physical injury.

When you are internally wounded, pain feels normal. You may not even recognize the difference if pain and destruction are all you have known and experienced throughout your life.

> We become comfortable in chaos and destruction, even
> when it hurts us, because we don't know any other way.

The emotional impact of hurtful words or name-calling can be even deeper than physical abuse. Voices linger in our heads, and emotional experiences stay in our hearts and resonate throughout our bodies.

Verbal and emotional abuse is directed at us personally, so it penetrates our psyche and physical senses, leaving a lasting impact. The painful memories remain with us long after the words are spoken.

But why do we allow abuse to happen? Why do we tolerate others hurting us? The main reason is that we feel helpless and powerless. We were not trained, and no one taught us how to defend ourselves or speak up for ourselves growing up.

If you grow up in a destructive, hurtful, hostile, or abusive home, as I did, you carry those traumas with you from that environment. As a result, you tend to recreate the same type of environment with similar kinds of people — because it feels familiar, and it is the life you know.

This pattern continues until you become aware of it, come to terms with it, and begin to heal. Another factor is that many of us have very low or even zero self-esteem and little willpower to stand up or speak up for ourselves, because we have lost our own voice or the ability to fight for ourselves.

We may believe that we are unworthy of love, respect, or care, so we allow others to disrespect or mistreat us. And we continue to allow it repeatedly, because this is where we feel familiar and comfortable — even if it is painful. Painful love becomes our normal.

We accept hurtful name-calling because it reflects how we see and value ourselves. We allow others to treat us in ways that please them, even while it hurts us.

As codependents, sometimes tolerating abuse becomes one of the ways we try to feel better — hoping that the person will give us the attention we seek and emotionally depend on them for. This is one of the many characteristics of codependency.

I had to face this truth when I realized that I had been allowing everything to happen, "hoping" to receive the attention that would comfort my needs to feel better.

When I recognized my own participation in abusive relationships, I understood that I may have been half-asleep or unconscious in my responses to what was happening.

Yet, knowing that I was physically present, I am responsible for my years of participation — for tolerating and allowing the abuse to continue.

This is one of many common stories about abusive relationships. One person feels helpless or powerless, while the other is the manipulator and abuser. The helpless often become the victims, believing they played no role in the situation.

But the reality is that, whether we are aware or conscious enough to see what is happening, we are still staying in the relationship and physically present.

In that way, we are participating. By tolerating the abuse, accepting the way the other person treats us, and allowing it to happen repeatedly, we gradually lose our ability and capacity to stand up for ourselves.

We victimized ourselves by placing all the blame on the other person. Until we become aware of our own participation and behavior, we will continue to attract and recreate the same life dynamics with other people.

If you are currently involved in a very dysfunctional or abusive marriage or relationship, ask yourself honestly: What role am I playing? What am I participating in that has put me in this situation?

Awareness and acceptance of what is happening within you and around you can be the beginning of change — and the first step on your journey to healing.

CHAPTER 4

WHY I KEPT RELIVING AND RE-EXPERIENCING MY PAST LIFE

I journeyed through life for thirty-nine years carrying a great amount of psychological, emotional, and physical trauma accumulated from countless traumatic and horrifying life events — especially my childhood experiences.

Not once did I look back to remember or revisit those painful memories, until a panic attack forced them to the surface. That powerful awakening brought forth all the unconscious traumas I had been carrying — traumas I never knew were still very active within me.

I had walked through life bearing the effects of these traumas up to that moment of awakening. I lived reacting to them, existing in a state of severe, unconscious depression. I kept recreating my past experiences in my present life, reliving my past over and over — all without awareness.

Only after that powerful lightning of awakening did I
realize that I had been sleepwalking through life.

My life had been a never-ending chain of painful and traumatic events, and I had been carrying the impact of those experiences unconsciously — until it all got activated. I developed multiple "disorders," and they all finally surfaced at once, haunting me simultaneously in the depths of my depression.

I grew up in a very hostile and violent home and was severely abused and mentally tortured as a child and raped multiple times - and all of these life events occurred while I was watching, participating, and responding unconsciously.

I had been half asleep until that moment of awakening. My crippling depression eventually led me to uncover every piece of trauma that had kept me trapped in darkness, pain, and sorrow.

As I began recalling and revisiting my past experiences, I was confused about how everything had happened while my eyes were wide open and I was physically present.

Then I realized that, yes, I was physically present — but I was lost and unconscious. I was so out of touch and so detached from the reality of what was happening within me, around me, and what others were doing to me.

I remember very vividly the moment I recognized my own behavior, mirroring my mother's severe codependency, and how my mother and I were behaving very similarly in our marriages.

I felt a profound sense of recognition during flashbacks, watching myself tolerate abuse — just as I had watched my mother in very similar scenarios when I was around six years old.

I also remember acting and behaving like my mother when I was put in the position of caring for my older children on my own after my first divorce. That was the moment I realized I was seeing myself as my mother. I was literally reliving and recreating the life of my parents.

I married two different men who shared the same personality traits and behaviors as both my father and my brother. Memories of my past were triggered when both of my ex-husbands behaved very similarly to my father and brother, simultaneously.

I married two men who felt so familiar, as if they had always been in my life. Their behaviors activated my unconscious traumas and, in a way, became a guiding path — helping me remember those parts of my past and eventually heal from them.

As I recalled my childhood memories and experiences, the more I realized just how similar both of my ex-husbands' personalities and behaviors were to my father and brother. This familiarity made it as painless as possible for me to relive my past and bring my unconscious trauma to the surface.

Seeing my father's past behaviors mirrored in my ex-husbands as I healed — and watching them act so unconsciously — became a truly profound healing experience. It was something anyone can experience through deep self-awareness and inner work.

It felt as if I was simultaneously witnessing my past life within my present life, becoming fully awake and conscious of both. The realization of how closely past and present events were connected was deeply powerful and transformative.

This was also the moment I recognized that much of my trauma had finally begun to release from my body, because I felt emotionally detached from those patterns and people.

The psychological and emotional trauma of my past surfaced intensely and all at once — so vividly that the memories felt present in my body and mind as I consciously brought them to the surface, to heal them.

I came to experience and understood the resilience of being human and what true courage really feels like — the courage that had been taken from me by every traumatic life event, yet returned when I needed it most.

Being in severe depression felt like a "Test of Death" — as if I were buried alive, gasping for air and summoning every ounce of physical and emotional strength just to survive. At the time, I could not understand what I was trying to escape from.

Only later did I begin to identify the deep, underlying traumas attached to my depression — what are often described as the "multiple symptoms" of depression.

The powerful impact of severe depression kept me curious, which eventually led me to recognize many of the past traumas hidden beneath it. The more I became aware of these traumas, the more memories of my past came back to life simultaneously, often through constant flashbacks.

Sitting in the agony and feeling every bit of psychological and emotional pain in the depths of my depression, I was able to bring years of unconscious traumas to the surface and become fully aware of them.

I learned to sense and recognize even the subtlest traces of severe depression and what they revealed about my inner wounds.

Depression made me understand that pain **is** and **will always** be a part of being human, for as long as we are alive. I had never truly understood the real existence of severe depression until I experienced it.

And because of that powerful experience and how it affected me, I was driven to seek my own answers.

Eventually, I discovered the underlying roots of my depression — which led me to heal myself, not just the symptoms, but the source of it.

> Depression is a reaction or manifestation of our unconscious psychological and emotional traumas. Most people experience depression at various levels, depending on their age and life experiences.

True healing can only come from the individual experiencing it — by becoming aware of their condition, understanding its roots, responding consciously, and allowing themselves to heal deliberately and naturally.

I know that there are many modern treatment options to heal psychological wounds — what I call the "shortcuts" or the easy way out. Based on my personal experience with healing, I would not choose any other path than reliving or re-experiencing the past.

By doing so, I not only heal myself, but I also heal those around me by gaining a deeper understanding of my own wounds.

The wisdom of healing lies in the process — in the journey itself. If you want to truly understand yourself and master every part of who you are, you must be willing to take this path and do the work.

This means revisiting your past life events and re-experiencing the psychological, emotional, and physical impacts of those events — until you become fully conscious and aware of your traumas.

This process allows you to understand yourself and the root causes of your internal suffering. When I began my healing journey, I sometimes felt lost as I revisited my painful past.

The more I brought those memories to the surface and became aware of them, the clearer I could connect the dots.

I began to recognize how my current actions and behaviors were directly linked to my past traumas. I can't empathize this enough that; Depression is a Manifestation of Accumulated Traumas.

And those who have experienced multiple painful or traumatic life events, are the most likely to experience severe depression at some point — or may already be living in a state of severe depression without realizing it.

Every person who shared their story with me about their journey through depression had grown up in dysfunctional homes and experienced some form of abuse or traumatic life events.

Many of these individuals also struggled with addiction, self-destructive behaviors, or being abusive or hurtful to themselves or others.

I witnessed many people battling addiction as a way to cope with their struggles. They may have known they were hurting themselves and others, yet they felt powerless to control their destructive urges. This lack of control often stems from unconscious trauma driving their behavior.

Not knowing the root cause of our behaviors or depressive experiences is what keeps us trapped in pain and maintains the state of depression.

My childhood and unconscious traumas were the driving forces behind my current life. They were like a dark cloud in the sky, blocking me from seeing things clearly. My panic attack activated it all, and I became conscious and fully aware of my internal state.

Darkness was where I lived for thirty-nine years. "Hate was my happy, and pain was my love." Recognizing and understanding the roots of my depression provided me with the answers I needed.

Now, when I get triggered, I can now easily identify which part of me is being affected. If it stems from a trauma, I look back at my past and remember the occasions or the person who caused it.

Very often, what triggers my trauma is the similar behavior or actions of someone in the present, or a life event that reminds me of my past.

Revisiting and remembering my past as often and as much as I could tolerate was a major part of my healing—and it still is, because healing is a lifelong journey.

In the depths of my depression, as I gained more awareness of what I was going through, I realized that I had been unconscious for most of my life.

Other people were running my life because I was half asleep. When I finally woke up and became aware of my past traumas, it felt as though I had no idea how I arrived at my current life or how I had created it.

I kept reliving the life I learned at home, and I carried both of my parents' identities for the first thirty-nine years of my life.

I married unconsciously and recreated a married life that felt familiar and comfortable to me. I became a mother and a wife and tried to build my own family based on my past traumas and life experiences.

How I parented my own children mirrored exactly how my mother had parented us. Reliving my parents' marriage through my own two marriages helped me understand their relationship more deeply.

My compassion immediately extended to them. Understanding my own life's journey and where I came from is where I found my own identity as an individual.

When you understand your own pain and suffering, you naturally develop the ability to understand the pain and suffering of those around you.

Most people are good by nature, but many carry unconscious pain. They often pass these experiences down from one generation to the next — a cycle known as generational trauma.

It is only when we recognize these continuing chains of trauma that we can break free from them and detach from the familiar pain and suffering that keep us trapped in depression.

When you begin to wonder why you cannot seem to "get it," no matter how much you try to be a better person, it is often because you are carrying unconscious trauma — and you are automatically responding or reacting from those traumas.

You will continue to make the same mistakes and may even pass that trauma onto your children. This cycle continues until someone recognizes the patterns, decides to heal, and breaks free from it.

My repetitive experiences helped me recognize these patterns and my willingness to step out of familiar and comfortable pain was what broke the chains and freed me completely.

After years of deliberate, conscious healing, my past traumas no longer hurt me emotionally or control my behavior.

They are now just memories — the psychological, emotional, and physical impacts are gone. I am free from them.

CHAPTER 5

THE COMMON AND THE UNCOMMON TYPES OF DEPRESSION

Out of curiosity and a desire for answers about my own journey through depression, I began observing people who had experienced—or were still experiencing real depression.

In my interactions with clients, family members, and friends, a few were willing to share their darkest experiences with depression.

Three of them had been struggling with it for over twenty years and could not find a way out of that darkness. Why? Because they were not aware of the roots of their condition.

Not one of them had any understanding of past life event traumas. These individuals were highly educated and intelligent men and women, yet they had no clue what was happening within themselves.

Two of them had been seeing therapists for years, yet they had not — and perhaps may never — come to the conclusion that their childhood history plays the biggest role in their long journey with depression, and what keeps them stuck in that state.

These individuals are in their forties and fifties, and I conducted this observation to confirm that depression is a manifestation or reaction to unconscious past traumas.

COMMON DEPRESSION

Charlie, 56: Charlie served in the military for over twenty years and spent a significant portion of that time on the battlefield. After retiring, he immediately began experiencing PTSD and severe depression, which I believe stemmed from a combination of battlefield trauma and unresolved childhood traumas. Despite years of counseling and medication, he realized that none of it was helping him feel any better, but he is determined to take control of his mental health. So, he decided to return to exercising and adopt a healthy, active lifestyle. However, despite his conscious efforts, he is still haunted by traumatic memories. The memories that dominate his mind are primarily those from the battlefield—the most recent and intense experiences he endured. Charlie remains unaware of his childhood traumas, and until he becomes conscious of these unresolved issues - his unresolved past will continue to influence his depression, behavior, and present-day choices and experiences.

Terry, 55: Terry is a very smart woman and incredibly bubbly to be around. However, when I spent more time with her in situations where alcohol was involved, I quickly noticed that she was dealing with something deep. She tried to hide it in every way she could—until a few drinks caused her to lose complete awareness and forget herself entirely. I noticed that substances were where she found comfort or surrendered herself. She used them to numb her pain—to forget—until she became very unconscious. I remember talking to her about depression; the word itself triggered her, and she strongly avoided the topic. Terry is a clear example of someone living in a state of deep depression without being fully aware of it—or perhaps being too afraid to face it. Instead, she searches for every possible way to cope, avoid, or escape it, whether through promiscuity, drugs, alcohol, or other self-destructive behaviors.

UNCOMMON DEPRESSION

Reena, 55: Reena did not experience abuse or any type of traumatic experiences growing up. She is married with children and has endured her husband's betrayals throughout their marriage, suffering depression caused by years of his deception, betrayal, and psychological and emotional abuse. Like many people I know—both men and women—Reena tolerated her husband's behavior and stayed in the marriage to protect her children. But unlike many who suffer from depression due to past trauma or unresolved unconscious issues, Reena does not have underlying childhood traumas; her depression stems primarily from her current life situation. She was able to overcome her depression and recover from the impact of her husband's behavior when he recognized the harm he had caused and changed his ways. Reena was able to remain calm and stable while living with her own depression, holding onto the hope that her husband would eventually change and that her struggles would eventually end. She confronted her depression consciously, acknowledging both its causes and the factors that were keeping her trapped in it.

Since Reena did not grow up wounded or traumatized, I noticed that her demeanor is the complete opposite of those who did—myself included. She is calm, grounded, and highly self-regulated.

As opposed to being restless, unstable, aggressive, or self-destructive, Reena maintained her composure. Had she been deeply wounded and carried unresolved unconscious traumas, she would not have been able to remain steady for decades while living in a painful marriage.

She was aware enough to understand the causes of her depression and fully recovered once her marital situation improved—able to forgive and move on.

Reena is one of the rare cases of someone who suffered depression and bounced back because her depression had no underlying roots in past trauma.

DEPRESSION IN BORDERLINE PERSONALITY DISORDERS

Jim, Patty, Frank, and Davis, were diagnosed with Narcissistic Personality Disorder, Bipolar Disorder, and Adult ADHD and are also dealing with multiple types of addictions. This makes them more depressed and more unstable, with behaviors marked by constant mood swings and frequent shifts in personality.

Most people would notice them as being "very different" in the way they behave and interact with others. From my observations, it is clear that they are significantly less conscious or largely unaware, which I believe contributes to why their journey through depression tends to be longer and more difficult than for others.

I also noticed that people with Borderline Personality Disorder are less likely to help themselves, seek help, or cooperate in their own healing.

> **Jim, 47:** He has battled severe anxiety, depression, and multiple addictions for more than twenty years. Jim is an overt narcissist on the high spectrum, and most people notice him for being different in the way he does things—often exceeding what most would consider "normal." After observing Jim for some time, I could see his deep-seated self-destructive behaviors, particularly his addictions. I often witnessed him lose control in an instant, becoming completely unconscious of his actions—as if he were swept away by a force of nature, carried off without awareness, and gone.

Patty, 45: Patty is one of the smartest women I know, yet also one of the most self-destructive. She was diagnosed with Bipolar Disorder (Manic-Depressive Disorder). After spending considerable time with her, I could easily tell that she was in a deep depressive state. However, she was aware of what she was experiencing internally, voluntarily sought help, and began taking medications. After weeks on medication, nothing seemed to change. She continued living a very depressed life and behaving compulsively. Her instability and highly complex personality—which can shift from minute to minute—are easy to detect if one pays attention, and most people would consider it "abnormal."

Frank, 51: Frank is dealing with Adult ADHD and is always jumpy, anxious, and hyper—so much so that I call him a "roller coaster." He has overcome his drug and alcohol addictions and believes he has also navigated his journey with depression in his own way. Frank has also battled major depression and generalized anxiety disorder (GAD) and is aware of his conditions, yet he believes there is no cure for depression. As a result, he has learned to live with it, functioning in his daily life while constantly feeling depressed, restless, and anxious. Frank has learned to embrace his hyperactivity, restlessness, and unpredictable nature. You can never fully anticipate his behavior from one moment to the next. One minute he is high and happy; the next, he may unconsciously slip into a dark, down, and depressed state.

Darren, 61: Darren is a sadistic narcissist on the high spectrum, who seems to derive satisfaction from seeing others hurt—both directly and indirectly through gaslighting, emotional abuse, and manipulation. It is disturbing to witness when you are aware of it because he deliberately targets people. Darren has an intense personality and is extremely unconscious, out of control, hot-tempered, and highly conflict personality. He thrives on conflict and appears to take pleasure in seeing others break. Yet Darren is also one of the most depressed and sorrowful individuals I have encountered. His constant targeting of others seems to be his way of coping with his own inner pain.

Charlie, Terry, Jim, Patty, Frank, and Darren are all self-destructive and afraid to be alone long enough to confront their unconscious behaviors. Instead, they run from their pain, numbing it through self-destructive actions or by hurting those around them.

- **Jim** turns to gambling, alcohol, sex, and food addiction for comfort.

- **Charlie** channels his pain into various physical activities.

- **Terry** seeks comfort through people-pleasing, drugs, and alcohol.

- **Patty** turns to sex and promiscuity.

- **Frank** has accepted that being depressed and anxious is simply a way of life.

- **Darren** targets vulnerable people to hurt and control.

They are all in a state of depression, each suffering internally for different reasons. If you are attentive enough, you can easily notice how unconscious they are. Until they become aware of their unconscious traumas, they will remain bound by them.

The more I observe people and explore depression, the more common it becomes. While the experience is unique to everyone, the common roots are the same: unconscious trauma, or unconscious pain and suffering.

The intensity and severity of depression depend on a person's age, upbringing, and the amount of trauma they have endured and accumulated throughout their lives.

Much like where I once was, these six individuals are all dealing with what are commonly referred to as the "symptoms" of depression.

Their unconscious behaviors directly reflect their internal state. They try to function in their lives as best they can, but their actions are driven by unresolved trauma.

Acting and behaving unconsciously, they continue to self-destruct and remain depressed. And this will persist until they become conscious of their aimless, unconscious actions and behaviors—and take steps to heal themselves.

CHAPTER 6

MY TRUTH ABOUT DEPRESSION

Depression took me to the darkest side of life, and my profound experience with it allowed me to see and understand the difference between light and darkness. It gave me the power to choose which path to take as I battled against it.

You can be your own enemy or your own ally when fighting depression. You can allow yourself to remain sick and depressed, or you can choose to rise and become your own savior. This is what it truly feels like to battle real depression.

You often feel as if you just want to close your eyes and go to sleep because you are constantly exhausted. It feels like you have nothing left inside you to keep fighting something you don't even fully understand.

Yet the truth continues to speak silently but powerfully, telling you that everything is your choice—and that you already have the answers and internal resources to help yourself rise above it.

To fight or not to fight—whatever you decide, you are the only person who will face the outcome of that decision. Depression is an intensely personal experience, one that only those who have endured it, are enduring it, or will endure it can truly understand.

We are the only ones who can grasp the meaning of every subtle pain that comes with this condition human called **depression**.

The moment I recognized that I was battling severe depression—and understood it as nothing more than a natural human condition—I resisted every urge to seek medical help, because I believed I could face it on my own.

I refused to let anyone convince me that I was "very ill" and needed to numb myself with medications that would only suppress the symptoms or dull the pain of depression—eventually leaving me trapped in it.

I chose the higher road—the unknown path of self-healing—and my willingness to do whatever it took to help myself made it possible. Self-healing became my daily mission, no matter how small the progress.

Some days were more excruciating than others, as facing my truths and digging into the painful memories of my past was not something I wanted to do—or revisit.

But knowing that my past trauma was the root cause of my severe depression and destructive habits, actions, and behaviors, I was willing to endure it all once more by revisiting those experiences. I did this so I could understand myself better, help myself heal, and ultimately be free from unnecessary pain and suffering.

As I came to know myself better, I was able to heal the parts of me that had been injured, tortured, terrorized, and traumatized. The profound and powerful impact of my severe depression made me very curious to understand what it was truly about.

As brutal as the experience of severe depression was, my curiosity guided me to keep fighting and searching for answers. One of the first things I noticed was my heightened awareness of my entire body and the sudden feeling of physical paralysis—even though I had lived a very active life.

Experiencing severe depression awakened my awareness and led me to a profound realization of what it truly means to feel both "whole" and "empty."

I came to understand that I had felt empty for most of my life. All I had was my physical body moving through the world while I remained internally wounded, hollow, and disconnected.

Self-healing took everything I had, because healing requires immense inner courage—your willingness to endure the entire healing process is what will ultimately set you free.

Freedom and liberation come together when you let go of the pain and suffering you are carrying or holding onto. So, release them and begin your own healing journey.

Medicating—or what I call "numbing" the symptoms of depression, is not a cure for depression. Based on my personal experience, I truly believe that medication alone cannot pull someone out of depression or fully heal a person from it.

Medications can only provide temporary relief. I had endured decades of psychological and emotional trauma from multiple abusive and traumatic life events—and I had no awareness that my entire internal system was still trapped in the past.

My depression was demanding my attention, urging me to wake up. After years of longing and yearning to feel better, and with the maturity I had gained, I was finally ready to confront it all.

I suffered from severe Complex Post-Traumatic Stress Disorder (CPTSD), caused by decades of painful and horrifying life experiences.

During my journey through severe depression, my trauma was simultaneously trying to wake me up. It felt as though something inside me was desperate to be released.

> I was numb and had lost my senses from the weight of severe depression. There were sounds, but I could not hear them. There were colors all around me, yet I could not distinguish them. Everything appeared gray and shadowed. Food lost its taste, and I felt no emotion other than a heavy numbness.

It didn't matter whether it was night or day because I felt as if I were always in darkness, no matter how bright and sunny it was outside. I withdrew from others and felt isolated, terrified, and very alone.

I stopped talking about what I was going through once I realized that many people around me were also moving through life without direction—lost, hurt, empty, and helpless.

Deep inside, I knew that no one could ever prescribe the right medication to heal my condition—because only I truly understood what I was experiencing within.

Depression is invisible, yet incredibly powerful. It kept me feeling paralyzed until I became aware of it. I felt helpless and powerless until

I discovered the profound dignity that comes from facing the battle of severe depression. By sitting still in the agony of its effects, I found the beginning of my own healing.

By feeling every subtle sensation of severe depression in every cell and tissue of my body, I came to understand something deeply profound about myself. The invisible power of depression is something I still cannot fully explain or put into words.

The experience was so powerful, so unique, so profound, and so intimate—there are not enough words to describe it. The magnitude of that experience is something only I can truly understand.

> The profound feeling of being severely depressed gave
> me the ability to deeply sense the light and darkness in
> my everyday life. It is subtle, yet unmistakably clear and
> profoundly loud.

Having experienced severe depression and emerged from it naturally, my conviction about depression became crystal clear: most people exist in some state of depression, to one degree or another. Depression is simply part of being human.

Most of us will experience some form of depression—consciously or unconsciously. Those who endure severe, clinical, or major depression are often the ones who have suffered traumatic life events.

Understanding the root cause of our personal journey through depression is the only way to protect ourselves from its return, when another unwanted or unexpected life event threatens to pull us back into that state.

Examining depression from all angles and dimensions—especially understanding its roots—and committing to heal ourselves is the only true way out.

By studying every part of yourself and examining your life—from the day you were born to the present—you not only learn how to deal with depression, but also begin to heal unresolved traumas, transforming your life into something beyond belief.

"Healing unconscious and unresolved traumas—the roots of depression—is the cure for depression."

As I continued to heal, I began to notice my depression slowly lifting. Gradually, I started feeling better each day until I felt "normal" again, and the world around me became brighter and clearer.

My head began to feel lighter, and my love for exercise became enjoyable again. I grew increasingly conscious and aware of what was happening within me and around me.

Most people are unaware that they are in a state of depression. It manifests in many forms through unconscious behaviors and self-destructive patterns, such as addictions, self-hatred, or other self-numbing behaviors.

In my healing journey, I recognized that most people are literally living in pain. The deeper I understood my own journey through depression, the more I felt challenged to go even further—searching for answers beyond the obvious symptoms of depression. Until I discovered this:

When you sit with your depression long enough and are willing to dig deep, you will encounter a part of yourself somewhere in that darkness. Confronting this part of yourself requires immense inner courage, which is why most of us run away.

This part of ourselves feels so foreign and unfamiliar that it can be terrifying. It is like meeting another person who has lived inside you all this time—the person you have been avoiding or are afraid to face.

This part of you is ready to give you nothing but the truth: the brutal truths most of us do not know about ourselves—our past which we've been avoiding confronting.

The unconscious part of ourselves, and our dark, unresolved pasts, are waiting—longing, crying, and seeking answers and resolution.

All my life, I was running away from that other person who lived inside me—a person I never knew existed: the deeply hurt, broken, wounded, and traumatized self.

It was while sitting still in the darkest hours of my depression, feeling the agony of what it was trying to tell me, that I finally found the part of myself I had been running from. By listening to every subtle message of my depression, I discovered my own answers.

Nothing and no one—other than ourselves—can save us from our own internal suffering and struggles. Drugs, alcohol, fame, power, money, and all types of addictions can only numb our pain for so long. The more you run from yourself, the more damage you create within.

Sitting still, listening, and acknowledging your inner voices—the ones that are always speaking to you—is the only way to emerge from the darkness called depression. And only **you** can recognize and identify them.

UNDERSTANDING THE MEANING OF EVERYTHING

As I became more conscious of my past traumas, the pain intensified—because more memories began to surface, demanding to be confronted and processed.

I often asked myself, how could I not have stopped any of these events from happening? — but I already knew the answer: I simply did not know any better.

I was not aware or conscious enough to make different choices in my past. The paralyzing pain of depression forced me to face my past and my unconscious traumas, allowing me to become fully conscious and aware of them.

As I continued walking the unfamiliar path of healing, I slowly began to sense the subtle yet powerful reality around me and to see things as they truly were. Everything became clearer as I grew more conscious and paid closer attention to what was happening within me and around me.

I began to recognize the separation between the conscious and unconscious parts of myself. It felt as though I was being pulled between opposing forces—between light and darkness, awareness and unawareness—experiencing the collision of feeling physically paralyzed while simultaneously wanting to fly. The experience was so real and so profound that it was impossible to ignore.

This subtle yet powerful sense of awareness—inner knowing, instinct, or intuition—is something I have recognized since I was a little girl. However, I didn't have the understanding, language, or meaning for it when it spoke to me.

It was only during my journey through severe depression that I truly connected with it and finally understood what it was. The first time I ever experienced it so strongly—almost as if something were trying to hit me in the head to get my attention—was about two years before my depression began.

I found myself surrounded by groups of people under the influence of substances inside a club at four o'clock in the morning, while I was completely sober. As I watched them, I felt a powerful, wordless message rising within me, urging me to leave.

It only became truly clear when I was in the depths of depression, where I had no choice but to listen, even while feeling paralyzed.

> Awareness, intuition, gut feelings, instincts, or inner knowing—they are everything. They are always on point and never fail to give precise guidance, if we can recognize them within ourselves. They are our human nature, our internal compass, and our most powerful resource to help us navigate anything in life.

After years of deliberate healing, I sought to understand all the meanings and find the answers to what I was experiencing—including the nature of why hurt people hurt people.

When I realized that confronting the people who hurt me were no longer an option, the first question I asked myself was: Who are these people, and how are they different from me? The answers appeared in glimpses of memories from my past life experiences.

I remember breaking down in tears while studying addiction and hearing the struggles of many addicts trying to overcome it. My thoughts immediately went to my father, who battled severe alcohol addiction until he became gravely ill—and ultimately lost his life to it.

I could not fully relate to what he was going through until I understood why addicts do the things they do. My anger and resentment toward my father transformed into compassion, which I longed to express—if only he could have waited for this moment.

He was fighting for his life in a hospital bed while I was fighting to survive my own depression.

Studying and understanding the nature of every person who hurt me healed and freed me—because understanding became the path to all the answers. I put myself in each of their shoes and learned everything I could about my abusers and how I had attracted them.

This allowed me to understand where we all came from and how our paths collided, as if I was experiencing their struggles myself. Through this process, I came to know and understand every part of my own inner wounds, just as I came to understand my abusers and those who hurt me.

My resentment transformed into compassion as I understood them, no matter how brutal or callous they had been toward me. Understanding the pain of others became my own healing and my path to freedom from continued suffering.

The healthier I became, the more I recognized that most people are wounded and hurting in some way.

When I began to truly understand my own suffering and its roots, I learned to embrace the overall experience of psychological and emotional pain and discomfort. I learned to sit with it whenever it arises and ask myself why it is being presented to me.

Sometimes, it is merely a past memory triggered by a similar event in my current life. Other times, it is my present circumstances trying to teach me something or redirect me onto a different path. My emotions became a loyal guide, showing me where to go and which direction to take.

Healing taught me that pain will always be a part of us for being tender and alive. Pain and discomfort are signals that something is wrong, or that something we did was wrong—and they don't dissipate until we confront and resolve them.

The effect of depression on me was so profound and so personal that I could distinctly feel every sensation of it throughout my entire being. Depression can become your own guiding path to step out of the darkness and free yourself from unnecessary pain and suffering.

You will never truly understand the meaning of a "brighter life" until you lift yourself from the depths of depression, rise above your dark journey, and heal its roots.

> Depression is one of the darkest experiences life can present, yet it can also become the path to entirely new life experiences—if you are willing to do the work and refuse to let yourself be victimized by it.

Now I know for certain that, unless a person is born with psychological abnormalities, depression is the result of years of accumulated life traumas. This is the very nature of depression.

Clinical or major depression is real, and depression exists as part of the human experience—something we should acknowledge as part of being alive and learn to overcome as it arises, naturally.

Medicating the symptoms of depression will only keep a person trapped in it, because medication alone will never heal depression. Natural healing does. And we all possess the innate ability and capacity to endure the healing process.

Healing can be excruciating and very lonely journey. This is why many people remain in familiar pain and suffering. Healing is agonizing, but I was willing to face it all.

I was willing to endure everything once more to reach the other side of those dark pasts that had kept me imprisoned. I had to confront the parts of myself that needed closure and resolution so I could finally be free.

It is impossible to move forward and truly pursue happiness while carrying the heavy weight of painful memories and unresolved traumas. You need to bring them to the surface, become aware of them, and make peace with them.

Living freely is impossible if unresolved psychological and emotional traumas keep pulling us backward. We must all confront our pasts and make peace with them, so they can release us and allow us to move forward.

CHAPTER 7

TWO (2) TYPES OF DEPRESSION

Based on my personal experience with severe depression and my observations of other people's journeys, I have come to recognized and believe that there are two (2) types of depression:

1. **UNCONSCIOUS DEPRESSION** – caused by unresolved or unconscious trauma. People in this category often feel depressed around the clock. They tend to internalize their struggles because they may not understand what is causing their emotional pain and internal suffering. These individuals are often the ones who seek professional help, and many use medication or therapy in an effort to feel better.

2. **CONSCIOUS OR SELF-INFLICTED DEPRESSION** – individuals in this category are more aware of their behaviors and emotional patterns. They frequently talk about feeling "*depressed*" and may seek validation or attention from others. At the same time, they often resist or refuse professional help,

despite having access to support.

Example of Conscious or Self-Inflicted Depression:

Jessie 48. Jessie is a former client of mine whom I have known for many years. Throughout that time, I observed patterns of attention-seeking behavior, storytelling, and exaggeration.

He often walked around telling people how "depressed" he was and displayed depressive behavior primarily to gain attention.

After spending significant time observing him, I noticed consistent storytelling patterns and how changes in his behavior correlated with the reactions he received from others.

Unlike individuals experiencing genuine or unconscious depression, Jessie appeared able to shift his mood almost instantly. When he realized he was no longer receiving attention, he would abruptly come out of his self-inflicted depressive state.

True or unconscious depression is not something a person can simply turn off. Those who experience it cannot just "snap out of it."

The word **"simultaneous"** left a profound impact on me when my unconscious traumas began resurfacing, at the same time I became aware and conscious of them. This awareness led me to recognize my simultaneous power to choose.

For a long time, the heavy weight of severe depression always won. I repeatedly found myself back in bed—feeling stuck, helpless, and powerless—despite a strong desire to get up and move forward.

As I grew more conscious of what was happening within me, I began to identify my willpower, or conscious power—the inner force that emerged each time depression attempted to leave me paralyzed and physically immobilized.

Eventually, through ongoing inner struggle and reflection, I woke up to this reality: we all have the power to choose how we want to feel.

When you find yourself dwelling in negativity, you can simultaneously choose to focus on what feels better — simply by choosing a more empowering emotion.

Whenever I am triggered, I realize I am always standing between choices. Everything is already there, waiting to be consciously chosen, once I recognize this within myself.

We always have the power to choose our direction whenever we find ourselves struggling internally. Where we are in life, and the emotional state we are in, are the direct results of both our conscious and unconscious choices.

To become aware of both, you must deliberately pay attention to the pulling and tugging sensations within yourself that constantly try to immobilize you. These represent the conscious and unconscious parts of you that are continually interacting and often working against each other.

There are many things in our daily lives that keep us depressed without us even realizing it. I spent a great deal of time observing people to understand what I call **"Daily Depressants"**. Habits and behaviors that quietly keep people feeling low or disconnected from life.

Most of what keeps us depressed exists in our everyday routines. These are the things we do repeatedly that dominate our days and slowly trap us in cycles of misery, poverty, agitation, stagnation, and depression.

So, I have listed some of the most common causes of daily depressants that may be part of your everyday survival habits. Many of these examples may apply to you.

SOCIAL MEDIA ADDICTION (Facebook, Instagram, X, TikTok, YouTube, Snapchat, etc.)

This is number one on my list because social media has become an **"instant drug,"** an escape, and a quick fix for many people's daily survival. I was there myself at one point in my life.

Social media has become the **"go-to"** distraction for many people to escape life's discomforts — to ignore or avoid the unwanted realities of their lives.

The instant relief that comes from scrolling is so addictive that users often fail to recognize how damaging it can be to their overall health, especially their mental health.

The unhappier people feel, the more they tend to rely on social media to avoid confronting the root causes of their unhappiness.

Spending hours online every day can gradually push someone into a depressive state, especially through constant exposure to violence, negativity, and harmful content.

Part of my healing process was consciously observing what was happening in both my inner and outer world — including my own behavior and the behavior of others.

As I observed myself, I realized that social media had begun to dominate my daily life as an **escape** from facing the reality of what was happening around me.

I recognized that spending hours on social media every day was one of the contributing factors to why I remained depressed for so long.

I was constantly consuming violence, negative news, political conflict, and, for the most part, people's carefully curated and often pretentious online lives — lives we actually know very little about.

What we see and absorb from others can trigger comparison and self-judgment. This habit of comparing our lives to others can make us feel inadequate and unworthy, which can easily push us into a depressive state.

What we often fail to realize is that we are comparing ourselves to people who move through life wearing different disguises — hiding behind masks for many reasons.

Whether you are aware of it or not, when your attention is constantly on social media, you can become psychologically and emotionally trapped by absorbing large amounts of toxic content. Over time, this can seriously affect your health and overall well-being.

This can eventually lead to depression, obesity, and various forms of emotional and psychological stress. It is especially easy to be influenced when we are already feeling unhappy or vulnerable.

Below are some strategies that can help you overcome social media addiction and other electronic habits that you may be engaging in unconsciously or mindlessly — habits that could be contributing to your daily depressants.

- Replace unhealthy urges with activities that are positive and nourishing for you, because whatever we repeatedly focus on becomes our personal experience.

- Limit your time on social media and electronic devices that are not related to work or school, do not serve your growth, make you feel depressed, or harm your life and relationships.

If you absolutely need to be on these platforms daily for any reason:

- Unfollow or eliminate negative and toxic accounts that consistently post harmful or discouraging content and negatively affect your mood and daily quality of life.

- Avoid consuming or engaging with content that is emotionally draining, stressful, or depressing.

- Follow accounts that inspire, uplift, educate, and motivate you.

You will feel empowered by making positive changes every day, and you will notice an immediate improvement in how you feel when you let go of the things that make you unhappy, depressed, or unmotivated.

ARE YOU PART OF A DESTRUCTIVE OR TOXIC FAMILY DYNAMIC?

I know this firsthand: when the family environment is destructive, it can become a major source of daily distress, caused by constant psychological and emotional stress.

The closer we are to people, the harder it is to detach and walk away. I grew up surrounded by dysfunctional family dynamics and later found myself recreating the same toxic patterns in my own relationships — simply because I didn't know any other way to navigate them until I became aware.

Family relationships can be some of the most difficult to manage because of our deep-seated emotional bonds and attachments. One of the toughest situations is living with substance abuse, where everyone in the household is affected by one person's destructive behavior.

I know parents who spent years enduring psychological, emotional, and financial stress trying to save a loved one — an adult family member — to the point of complete devastation of the entire family.

Dysfunctional and toxic family relationships can be profoundly depressing because we naturally expect our family to be there for us — especially in moments of weakness, when we need support the most. It took me decades to find my own answers.

During the darkest period of my depression, my father passed away — and that was the moment I woke up to the reality of my entire family and where they were in their lives. I realized that even our own blood relatives will not always be there for us.

Not because they don't want to help, but because they lack the capacity to do so. Many of them are struggling themselves, needing the same help and resources that we wish they could give. Most people feel so helpless that they cannot even help themselves with their own struggles.

After years of healing, learning, and trying to understand why family members are often the first to let us down — and can be the most difficult to understand or forgive — I came face to face with a brutal truth: most of us are wounded in some way, and many people are simply in survival mode, trying to feel better.

Unfortunately, we often express that need in unhealthy ways. If pain is all we have experienced in life, we naturally express ourselves through pain as a coping mechanism, because we do not know any other way — until we heal and discover what it feels like to be internally healthy.

If family members do not understand or practice personal boundaries themselves, chances are they will neither respect nor understand yours. Over time, I discovered what I believe is the most peaceful solution for everyone.

The solution is to detach and stop participating in the destruction, choosing instead to remain at peace within yourself while allowing others to grow and learn their own life lessons.

When you find yourself involved with or surrounded by destructive family members, the best thing you can do is step away from the negativity and reflect — both on yourself and on how you may be participating in it.

Our life experiences are often the direct result of our own involvement in what is happening around us.

When we stop cooperating with or participating in someone else's chaos or destruction, they will eventually stop — or find other ways and different outlets to express themselves.

Unless they are minors or young children, adult family members — including your own adult children — must be allowed to learn life lessons from their own mistakes, poor choices, and bad decisions. Enabling is not helping; it's crippling.

This is not an easy decision to make, and it does not mean you are a heartless parent. Most of us grow, improve, and learn to navigate life through our own experiences and errors.

Your intuition will signal when you are ready to take this approach — often after you have done everything possible to help, and nothing seems to work.

Most people know what they are doing, and many act out to gain attention. With awareness, we can usually distinguish between someone misbehaving out of rebellion and someone who is truly in need of help, based on their psychological state and where they are in life.

Even when someone is not in the right state of mind, we cannot save anyone from their own life or personal struggles. Sometimes, the destructive person might even be you — creating conflict for those around you in an attempt to gain attention.

The harder you try to control or fix everything, the more depressed you may feel. Destruction only leads to more destruction — not just for you, but also for the people you love and care about.

As the American author, poet, and civil rights activist **Maya Angelou** said:

"If you don't like something, change it. If you can't change it, change your attitude."

ARE YOU CONSUMED BY WORRYING ABOUT OTHER PEOPLE AND THEIR OPINIONS?

I struggled with this for most of my life. It was a daily battle until I realized that worrying about others — including my entire family — was one of the main reasons I couldn't do what I truly wanted or move forward in life.

The mere thought of someone judging or misperceiving me would hold me back and leave me feeling immobilized.

After years of fighting this battle and obsessing over what people **might** think of me and my actions, I finally woke up to a simple truth: I was creating all the monsters in my head. I had been imagining unrealistic, frightening, and often impossible scenarios about what others were thinking.

The reality is that most people don't think about me — or even notice what I do — nearly as much as I imagine, because all of us are too busy with the thoughts and challenges of our own lives. In other words, we are rarely at the top of anyone else's mind.

Healing helped me recognize a deeply destructive mental habit that had fueled much of my chronic suffering: worrying about and fearing the opinions of others — even people I didn't know or care about.

When I finally became aware of this pattern, I realized that worrying about others' opinions often goes hand in hand with codependency, people-pleasing, low self-esteem, and a diminished sense of self-worth.

We base much of what we do on the approval of others because we fear that if we make a mistake, people will reject us — or we feel that we are simply not worthy.

I recognized in myself that this constant worry about others' opinions, perceptions, and judgments was driven by a crippling sense of inadequacy. It often led me to prioritize pleasing others over taking care of my own needs.

Most of my decisions were guided by other people — friends, family members, and even acquaintances I barely knew. That moment of realization gave me the answer to why I was always feeling depressed and constantly disappointed.

When we make life choices based on others, we unconsciously tie our happiness to their reactions or responses. Yet those people often have no idea that we are basing everything we do on them — to please them, gain their approval, be liked, or feel accepted.

When they fail to meet our expectations, we feel down, depressed, and disappointed. Often, we blame them or build resentment toward them, not realizing that the source of our suffering lies within our own need for external validation.

Unless we clearly communicate our intentions, desires, or expectations to others, we will never receive the outcomes we secretly hope for — from them or for ourselves.

The tendency to people-please can run deep, frequently developing from childhood patterns of prioritizing others' needs over our own.

It can also stem from a constant need for attention or validation — a desire to feel worthy, valuable, and assured that we matter.

So, starting today, whenever you catch yourself thinking about or worrying over other people, remember this: people are not paying as much attention to you as you are paying to them.

ARE YOU IN AN ABUSIVE OR DESTRUCTIVE MARRIAGE OR RELATIONSHIP?

This is a very common reason many people feel depressed, helpless, hopeless, or powerless. Some become chronically depressed after years of living in a destructive or painful marriage or relationship — often without even realizing it.

When destruction and dysfunction become a "normal" part of daily life, depression can become the default state of being. For those involved in abusive or toxic relationships, it often becomes a way of life.

It is nearly impossible to feel good or truly be happy when your life is filled with pain, destruction, and chaos.

If you are in any type of abusive relationship — whether verbal, emotional, sexual, or physical — you are likely to feel depressed most of the time.

Domestic violence, abuse, and a destructive home environment are not only damaging to you but also profoundly affect growing children, who absorb and internalize that environment.

Everything we and our children absorb at home carries over into our lives outside of it. Our actions, reactions, and decisions are often shaped by the emotional and psychological impact of that environment.

Your children may appear unhappy, irritable, or even act out at school because they are carrying the effects of what they experience at home.

Living in an abusive or destructive environment often means existing in a constant state of emotional heaviness — feeling low no matter how much you try to put on a happy face and pretend everything is okay.

How we feel inside inevitably shows on the outside, whether we are aware of it or not. Many people in abusive or destructive relationships remain because they feel afraid, ashamed, embarrassed, helpless, or powerless to leave or change the situation.

If you are in this situation, remember you have the power to choose — to stand up, to leave, and to go when you decide to. Nothing and no one can stop you from doing so, unless you are physically restrained.

You can leave, stop participating, and stop enabling, regardless of whether anyone agrees with you. We are responsible for our own happiness and well-being and to protect ourselves from any harm.

If you have children, the sooner you take action to change your life situation, the better — not just for yourself, but for their protection and well-being as well.

Remaining in an abusive or destructive marriage or relationship can gradually erode every part of you. Feeling depressed and in pain all the time is like being sick or constantly unwell — physically, mentally, and emotionally.

Until you change your situation or walk away, you may continue to harm yourself and, if you have children, potentially affect them as well.

Take a moment to sit with yourself and ask these questions, answering as honestly and thoughtfully as you can — because the truth sets us free.

- Is this relationship good for me, or is it serving me in any healthy way?

- What am I truly gaining from this relationship?

- What role am I playing in the abuse or dysfunction?

- Is my partner truly the cause of this, or am I contributing to my own misery by allowing or participating in the situation?

- Is there hope for improving this relationship if I am willing to change my own behavior for the better?

- Is my partner capable of recognizing their role in this situation?

- What are the real reasons I am staying in this relationship? Is it love? And if it is, is love alone enough to stay — or am I remaining because I feel helpless and not strong enough to leave?

- Am I staying in this relationship for the right reasons?

We are often stuck in painful situations because of our own denial — denying what we already know out of fear of facing the truth. If you take the time to sit with yourself and ask these questions, you may realize that you already have the answers you need to make the right decisions.

How you feel about a situation rarely lies. Start by taking care of yourself and prioritizing your own needs, because when you feel better, you think more clearly and make healthier choices.

Change does not happen overnight. But if you do not act today, you may wake up tomorrow in the same painful and discouraging situation.

Love yourself enough to seek happiness, and care enough about yourself to protect your well-being — because no one else can do it for you. The sooner you make that decision, the closer you are to finding the right path.

A path where things feel aligned — and where one courageous action or decision can lead you toward a happier, healthier life, and eventually to the right person and relationship.

ARE YOU OVERWEIGHT OR STRUGGLING WITH OBE-SITY?

If you are living with obesity, it can be a significant contributor to depression and may keep you trapped in a persistent low mood.

This struggle can feel like a daily battle with yourself — especially if your weight affects your physical functioning or overall well-being. It is difficult to feel good about ourselves when we know that we are harming our body, regardless of the reason.

I have worked as a health and fitness coach for over twenty years, living and breathing fitness and practicing proper nutrition as a way of life. From my experience, a common cause of obesity or weight gain is **overeating** — consistently consuming more than the body needs — rather than poor nutrition or lack of exercise alone.

When I began training clients, I quickly noticed a common pattern among those who were overweight or struggling with their health: it often stemmed from dissatisfaction with themselves or their personal lives.

Our urges and cravings to overeat are frequently emotional responses to what is happening within us. From my own experience, when I don't feel good about myself, I tend to overeat because food provides instant relief and temporary comfort — which is usually followed by regret.

Unhealthy eating habits are often driven by our emotional state. Nearly three decades in the fitness industry, while training clients and hearing their personal stories, I noticed a consistent pattern: the root cause of obesity and being overweight was often unhappiness.

This unhappiness can stem from many sources — unhealthy relationships, unfulfilling jobs, financial struggles, dissatisfaction with physical appearance, and more.

Over time, this unhappiness can evolve into self-hatred, which often leads to destructive choices. Overeating may become a form of self-destruction, emotional numbing, self-loathing, or even self-harm.

Trying to escape the reality of what is happening in our lives — whether by going to the gym or hiring a personal trainer — will not resolve the underlying issues. Until we address the core problems and the real reasons why are where we are, no external solution can bring lasting change.

It is easy to focus on our physical appearance and believe that the problem lies solely in what we see on the outside. As a result, we often seek help for that reason, when in reality the issue is rooted in how we feel inside — something only we can recognize and address.

Many people who hire trainers or seek professional help achieve their weight or fitness goals, only to stop once they reach them. The moment they stop working with a trainer, they often return to their previous habits — and may even gain more weight than before.

Why? because the real root causes of their unhealthy eating and self-destructive habits have never been addressed.

So, before you begin this journey, take a moment to sit quietly and honestly ask yourself: Where am I psychologically and emotionally? or what is truly going on in my life?

You will soon recognize many of the reasons that have been driving you to overeat, draining your energy, and keeping you in a state of depression.

The moment you start improving your life and the way you feel about yourself, everything begins to change. Our negative psychological and emotional states often fuel unhealthy eating habits and self-destructive behaviors.

You don't need to hire a trainer or get a gym membership to begin this journey. Change begins the moment you are ready to take responsibility and act on it. Start with complete honesty with yourself.

Start by cutting out one type of unhealthy food or sugary drink each day and begin moving your body — even if it's just for ten minutes a day. This simple step can make a big difference because it's about breaking the bad habits you've grown comfortable with, even though they don't serve you.

No matter how small the changes, as long as you are consistent and committed, they will add up to significant results over time.

You don't need to completely change your diet at first. Focus on developing new habits by resisting cravings whenever they arise. Resist the urge to sit or lie down if you have the option to walk around — every small act of resistance strengthens your self-discipline and brings you closer to your goals.

Staying physically healthy and capable is a way of life if we want to live a happier, more fulfilling life. We need to take care of our bodies so we can feel better about ourselves. When we feel good internally, we can handle daily life more easily and enjoy it more fully.

If your condition is influenced by patterns from previous generations, you have the power to break the cycle for yourself and your family. By doing so, you can also inspire your loved ones to take care of themselves and make positive changes in their lives.

Don't discount the small progress you make. If you are committed to doing what is necessary, big changes will eventually come through consistent effort and small daily sacrifices.

Give yourself the time and pace you need. As long as you are consistently making progress every day, change will happen, and you will start to feel lighter and better. Focus on small daily improvements while enjoying the process, rather than worrying about the unrealistic desired outcome or trying to perfect everything.

It's all about making small changes each day until these new healthy habits and ways of living become second nature.

There are many free and accessible resources online to support you along the way. In life, any meaningful change always begins with the willingness to do the work.

Love yourself enough and care enough about yourself not to stay where you are. If you don't start today, tomorrow you may wake up in the same state — feeling sluggish, heavy, and depressed all day.

Today is the time to begin. Start exactly where you are, doing what you can, with whatever resources you have.

ARE YOU CHASING THE WRONG PERSON OR PEOPLE?

This alone can keep you feeling deeply depressed, because life is fundamentally about relationships — we are social beings by nature. We naturally want to feel that we belong to a certain person, group, community, or circle of friends.

But chasing the wrong people — the wrong friends, partners, or groups — in search of acceptance, value, or appreciation can be exhausting and very discouraging. It becomes even more painful if they continually reject you, ignore you, or make it clear that you don't belong in their circles.

After decades of chasing the wrong people, I realized something important: most of us are chasing the same thing for the same reasons — happiness and fulfillment.

If you are chasing or waiting for a specific person, the energy you spend chasing, waiting, hoping, wishing, praying, or even crying is more than enough to keep you depressed.

Being so emotionally occupied with someone or something that drains you can have a lasting negative impact on your health. This long-term emotional strain can be a major contributor to your depression.

> Never chase or beg people for anything and never try to force anyone to do anything they don't want to do — because people respond best when acting from their own free will.

As the famous **American Actor Will Smith** said:

"Don't chase people. Be yourself, do your thing, and work hard. The right people — the ones who truly belong in your life — will come to you. And stay."

If we constantly look to others to feel complete, to feel better, or to be happy, we often end up attracting the wrong people. This happens because we draw the same energy from others who are seeking the same thing.

Relying on others for your happiness can leave you feeling depressed and unfulfilled, because you are attaching your sense of well-being to them. This chase never ends until you address the root cause.

We can never control what others do, and for this reason, you may continue to feel empty, unhappy, and even more depressed.

Never try to force yourself into any person, group, or community where you don't feel welcomed or accepted. Instead, take the time to sit quietly and reflect on why you feel the need to rely on others for your happiness.

Often, this longing comes from an empty space within us — and you won't recognize it if you keep running away from it.

> Nothing and no one outside of you can ever fill that emptiness. Only you truly know what it is, and only you can fill that void.

In the depths of my depression, I recognized what was missing — what I had been searching for, mistakenly believing that only "someone else" could fulfill it. When you learn to sit long enough and truly listen to your need for others, you will find the answer to that emptiness.

Soon, you will realize that what you have been longing for from other people has always been inside you. The next time you feel the urge to reach out or seek someone, sit with that feeling until the impulse passes.

We often rush to fill that emptiness, trying to escape the discomfort, and in doing so, we miss the valuable message it is trying to give us.

ARE YOU MEDICALLY ILL OR LIVING WITH PHYSICAL DISABILITIES?

As I was healing from years of severe psychological and emotional trauma, it took me a long time to recognize how much of that trauma had become trapped in my physical body — leaving me feeling physically paralyzed and very depressed. Only when I began consciously practicing the mind-body connection did I recognize that my trauma was lodged in my body.

I witnessed myself physically rising from those traumas. I went from feeling heavy, sluggish, and constantly exhausted to feeling light as a feather as my healing progressed.

One important insight I noticed was that the more I dwelled on or focused on my physical condition, the heavier and more burdened I felt.

Being in physical pain can also contribute to depression, especially when we fixate on our condition. My favorite quote, "**What you focus on, grows**," proves to be very true.

The more you focus on your pain, the more intense it feels. Conversely, the moment you shift your attention away from that pain, you may hardly notice that the discomfort has lessened — even if only for a few seconds.

I have many family members who were medically ill, and those who actively worked to help themselves were the ones who improved and lived longer.

The ones who were afraid to move, who didn't take steps to care for themselves, were the ones who repeatedly returned to the hospital — which, in some cases, ultimately led to premature deaths.

Our bodies are made to move — so the longer we remain immobilized, the weaker we become. We must use our willpower to help ourselves, no matter how painful, hopeless, or helpless we may feel.

You can still choose to see the brighter side of your condition. You can still choose to connect with the part of yourself that longs to feel better. Feel that good part of yourself — because it is there.

Notice that when you resist the pain or try to avoid feeling it, the discomfort only intensifies. Resistance delays your healing.

Believing that you may never get better keeps you stuck. Your desire to feel better is what drives real improvement. Your willpower is stronger than any part of yourself, and you are far stronger than you believe or think you are capable of.

You may not have given yourself the chance to cultivate that strength before — but now is the time to try. All the power you need is already inside you. We become exactly what we believe and what we command ourselves to do — or not do.

I am one of those people who avoids taking medication unless it is absolutely necessary. I have undergone multiple major surgeries, and I chose to experience the pain without masking it with pain relievers, because I wanted to feel my body's natural healing process.

As a result, I developed a high tolerance for physical pain. I truly believe that being attuned to what was happening inside my body helped speed up my recovery and prevented complications.

I lived most of my life physically active and full of energy. However, during the darkest period of my depression, I became intensely aware of what was happening inside my body. I constantly felt physically paralyzed, struggling to grasp even the smallest amount of energy.

After years of deliberate healing, I experienced many profound shifts — moments when something seemed to lift out of my body. These physical and emotional shifts were impossible to ignore, which motivated me to continue exploring and experimenting with my own healing process.

First Incident:
One day, I was under stress and noticed a sharp, shooting pain in my right shoulder. When I got home and lay down, I focused on the pain while consciously breathing in and out, fully feeling it. Fifteen minutes later, I got up, and the pain had completely disappeared.

At the time, I thought it might just be a coincidence, so I initially ignored what had happened.

Second Incident:
Later, I experienced stomach pain and went to see a doctor. After multiple tests and ultrasounds, the results came back "normal," yet I was still in pain. Then I remembered what I had done a few weeks earlier.

I decided to experiment again. I focused all my attention on the area of pain and began examining the current state of my life.

I soon realized that my stomach pain was linked to anxiety and constant worrying. The moment I adjusted my stress level; I woke up the next day feeling completely fine — the pain I had endured for weeks was gone.

It was truly magical to witness that I was literally healing myself physically — almost accidentally.

My healing journey began with many profound experiences that sparked a deep curiosity about what was happening to me. You might think this sounds crazy, but my entire healing process started simply because I was curious.

That curiosity led me to explore every possible answer I could find. This exploration then led to one miraculous experience after another.

I want to encourage you to try this very simple process yourself — and witness your own miracles or unexplainable healing experiences, even if only for a brief moment.

The main goal is for you to become fully aware of every part of your body. Begin by focusing on where it hurts and fully feel and experience the pain. You don't need to do anything drastic — all you need to do is start noticing every sensation in your body and paying attention to how you feel.

If you can, write down your observations each day. You can practice this whenever you feel any pain or discomfort. Do not ignore or resist the pain, and don't try to stop it. Simply feel it, direct your attention to it, and breathe in slowly as you experience the sensation. Then, let go and fully relax your body as you breathe out slowly.

Do this for five to fifteen minutes at a time and repeat whenever you feel physical pain or discomfort. Notice the subtle yet powerful effects it creates. You won't know the results unless you try — so go ahead, explore, and have fun with it!

No one else can heal our pain but us — because no one else can feel it or know exactly where it resides in our body. I have seen many people in physical pain who are too afraid to move, simply because they fear experiencing the discomfort.

This is also why many patients who undergo surgery remain on pain medications for years. They are afraid to feel the natural sensations in their body, so they live numbed, lifeless, or crippled by the effects of powerful medications. Their entire lives become controlled by these drugs.

I overcame my internal and external pains, that I once believed were impossible to heal — or that I wasn't even fully aware existed. It all started by being open to every positive possibility. My curiosity, experimentation, and exploration eventually led me to a place where I mastered every part of myself.

I became the master scientist of my own internal and external well-being, and I became my own healer — something I never knew I was capable of, or even that was possible.

The truth is, we all have that same ability and the capacity to endure anything and help ourselves navigate life's challenges.

Medications and a helping hand can only do so much. It is you who can redirect your focus to where you want it to be, helping yourself feel better each day. You can use your inner capacity to reject illness or physical limitations that try to keep you immobilized.

It is you who can tell yourself that you want to wake up tomorrow feeling at least a little better than today. Don't let the weak part of yourself convince you to stay stuck in that condition.

Even if you are physically limited, you can still choose how you experience your condition by changing your attitude or your responses to it.

Your will, strength, and courage are always within you, ready and always available whenever you need them. You are your own healer, and your healing begins with your willingness to help yourself.

ARE YOU A STRUGGLING SINGLE PARENT?

This alone can be a major source of daily stress and depression, as we try to manage everything on our own. The younger the children, the more time, attention, and care they require — and we often feel guilty, thinking we're not doing enough.

Most parents, myself included, feel that we are falling short because we want to give our children the best life possible.

After going through two divorces and becoming a single parent, I realized that we often beat ourselves up by trying to go beyond our abilities and capacity.

This constant striving can lead to a stressful and depressive life. By stretching ourselves thin to meet every need of our children, we often neglect our own well-being.

After my first divorce, I was completely unprepared for the sudden life changes of being a single mother to three young children. That was when I realized that I had not yet fully grown as a parent — and that I still needed to parent myself. It was overwhelming and terrifying, and I didn't know how to begin my new life.

No one is ever fully prepared for unwanted or unexpected life events. At the height of our emotions, we cannot think clearly or respond effectively to what is happening.

This became my daily source of depression until I made the choice to close my eyes and change the direction of my life, not knowing what would happen next.

None of us can predict what comes next. All we have is faith and trust — faith in the unknown and trust in our abilities and overall capacity to get through anything.

As parents, we often put our children first and ourselves last — when it should be the other way around. We need to prioritize our own needs in order to be better parents.

When our needs are met and we feel good about ourselves, parenting becomes effortless because we are not constantly seeking anything from others.

This allows us to give more to our children, and fulfilling our responsibilities as parents becomes more rewarding and enjoyable. Living every day under stress, trying to do more than we can handle, is energy-draining and can be very depressing.

I had to learn this the hard way: that in order to be a good and responsible parent, we must first be healthy, happy, and joyful. The energy we carry is passed on to our children, whatever that energy may be.

When we are miserable and unhappy, chances are we treat our children from that place — and children naturally respond to the energy and treatment they receive. In turn, they can become unhappy and distressed.

So, how can you unload some of the burden as an overwhelmed single parent?

- Take care of yourself first and foremost every day before attending to your children. Just like on an airplane, you are always instructed to put on your own oxygen mask before helping others.

- If you are struggling financially, exchange favors with trusted friends, neighbors, or family members for babysitting to save money — or offer babysitting to earn extra income.

- If you can afford it, hire a babysitter or use a daycare for a few hours so you can spend quality time attending to your own needs. It is not selfish to have some alone or "me" time — every parent needs it daily to recharge and maintain their well-being.

The examples above are just a few of the many things parents often forget to do to make parenting easier. The most important part of parenting is to care for yourself first and ensure that your own needs are met through consistent daily self-care.

When you do this, everything becomes more manageable and enjoyable — because you can think clearly and respond to your parenting responsibilities with greater ease.

ARE YOU GOING THROUGH DIVORCE OR SEPARATION?

I know for sure that divorce or separation can trigger self-inflicted depression and become a significant source of daily stress and emotional pain.

The process of divorce can involve years of suffering, especially if it is contentious and no one is willing to cooperate to make it as smooth and stress-free as possible.

Divorce has been proven to be one of the most damaging life events, affecting not only the parents but also children, extended family, friends, and the wider community involved in the family dynamic.

My two divorces had very different impacts on me because the relationship dynamics were not the same. However, both were deeply depressing — not only because of my own pain, but also because I felt for my loved ones, especially my children, who did not ask to be in this situation.

This alone can keep you in a dark place, trying to handle everything at once. The best approach is to stay present in reality, accept the situation as it is, and not lose your grip on what is happening.

When we are overwhelmed by heavy emotions, we often act irrationally. This is one of the main reasons why many divorce cases can take years to finalize — because people remain emotionally attached to the event.

It is completely normal to mourn the loss of a marriage or relationship that was important and meaningful to you. However, it is equally important to take full responsibility for your part in what happened. Regardless of who initiated the divorce or separation, both parties are affected negatively.

Failing to take responsibility and placing all the blame on the other person keeps you feeling victimized and depressed. No matter how painful it is, accept that the situation has happened — it is reality, and it cannot be changed.

Divorce is one of the most difficult life events to accept, no matter how stable or internally healthy you are. I know many people who never fully recovered from divorce or breakups.

They hope it didn't happen, blame the other person for everything, or wish the situation were different — and as a result, they remain stuck in a depressive state, feeling like a victim.

The sooner you take full responsibility for yourself; the sooner you can identify and understand the reasons why things happened and why they had to happen. Maintaining your dignity by standing strong for yourself, despite the pain and disappointment, will make it easier to navigate your situation.

It takes a sound mind and a strong heart to respond to events like this rationally. Many people remain heartbroken for years, some for decades, and some never recover, holding onto the belief that the "other person" caused it all or destroyed their life.

Refusing to take responsibility keeps them trapped in a victimized state. I experienced this firsthand with my first divorce. The longer you remain in this painful state, the harder it becomes to recover.

After three years of living in the agony of my past relationship, I began to wonder if I would ever get out of it. One day, I woke up to the realization that I was the one keeping myself in that state — by holding onto something that had happened years ago and no longer existed.

I recognized that I was experiencing the stages of healing simultaneously: rage, anger, blame, resentment, feelings of deception and betrayal, and deep victimization. These overwhelming, mixed emotions stirred my entire being to the point where I wanted to give up.

But knowing that I was the only one who truly understood what was happening inside me, I had to take ownership of it. I told myself that I would never allow myself to become my own enemy or defeat myself.

That powerful self-talk and inner conviction pulled me out of that state almost instantly. It was the truth speaking to me — and this time, I was finally ready to hear it.

I was finally willing to accept the situation after years of unnecessary pain and suffering. Even if we are victimized by another person or by unwanted life events or circumstances, it is ultimately our choice whether to remain a victim.

When we are in the height of our own emotional turmoil, we often fail to realize how our irrational actions and behaviors affect those around us.

If you have children, you don't want them to carry the memories of all the painful parts of what happened, because they can absorb that trauma as they grow. Often, it resurfaces later when they are old enough to confront you.

From my own experience and observations, children who grow up in destructive or negative environments often become destructive themselves, sometimes turning to self-destructive behaviors.

This can include drugs or other addictions as a way to express suppressed negative emotions absorbed from a toxic home environment. I was one of those children.

I felt completely lost, helpless, and alone in my own home, trapped in the destructive and dysfunctional environment my parents created.

I was raped and abducted while trying to run away from a home that was extremely hostile and violent. Feeling horrified and unsafe twenty-four-seven drove me to stow away and navigate life as a lost, vulnerable, and helpless young girl, searching for a safe home and people who could protect me.

Unfortunately, I ended up in even worse situations because I was so vulnerable, lost, afraid, helpless, and powerless.

ARE YOU OR THE OTHER PARENT ALIENATING YOUR CHILDREN?

Parental alienation is a form of emotional and psychological child abuse, where one parent belittles or vilifies the other parent in front of their children.

I know this from my own experience, as well as from clients and close friends, that co-parenting with a very difficult co-parent can be a major cause of daily depression.

Constantly battling and fighting for your rights as a parent is exhausting. This is a very common, yet often unseen, unnoticed, or unrecognized form of child abuse — usually caused by one parent's bitterness or resentment during or after a divorce or separation.

Some parents use their children to get back at the other parent, not realizing that this behavior harms their own children by teaching them to hate or oppose the other parent.

Parental alienation often damages children more than the divorce or separation itself. It occurs when a resentful parent manipulates the children to turn against the other parent. I want you to recognize and understand the following:

- Alienating your children from their own mother or father harms not only the children and the parent-child relationship but also your own relationship with them.

- Alienating your children teaches them to hate, which can later turn into hatred toward themselves and even toward you — often leading to self-destructive behaviors as a coping mechanism.

- Alienating your children from their mother or father fosters inner rage, as children often internalize their feelings and emotions.

- Teaching your children to go against their own mother or father damages their psychological and emotional health, because no child wants to "intentionally" hate their own parents.

As a severely abused child myself, I understand how parents' negative behaviors — whether intentional or not — can affect young children's psychological and emotional health.

Parental alienation is far more common than is publicly acknowledged, in part because this behavior is often very subtle and deceptive.

Parental alienation is especially prevalent in divorces or among parents who are constantly in conflict. This environment alone can be a major cause of persistent feelings of depression. Regardless of which parent is alienating the children, it is an extremely stressful and damaging situation for the entire family.

I never truly understood what parental alienation was until I experienced it with my own children. I constantly struggled to have peaceful time with them, while their father intruded, repeatedly taking away their attention during my parenting time.

It was incredibly depressing. When children have been heavily manipulated, trying to defend yourself or explain your actions often does not change their perceptions — whatever has already been instilled in them about you remains.

If you are dealing with a very difficult co-parent and your child or children are beginning to turn against you, this could be the start of parental alienation or manipulation.

The other parent — or even a new stepparent or partner — may be influencing your children to go against you, often driven by their own feelings of revenge or jealousy.

I have experienced this myself, and I have seen many parents do this to their children — often without realizing that they are hurting their own children more than anyone else.

Some parents intentionally put the other parent in a position where they appear powerless in front of the children, causing the children to perceive the other parent as the "bad guy."

I know a client and friend who is a very busy professional and has completely lost his emotional connection with his children — even though they all live in the same house and he is around them every day.

This happened because his spouse, who was the homemaker, influenced the children to reject their father, driven by her own unhappiness in the marriage.

I also know a close friend who is divorced, with the other parent living in another state, yet their child remains very close to both parents. Why? Both parents remain civil for the sake of their child and continue to cooperate and participate unconditionally in their child's life.

> Children's behavior toward their parents is a direct reflection of the relationship the parents have with each other.

Children raised in healthy co-parenting environments are generally happy and well-adjusted — and the opposite is also true. Children raised in destructive or hostile co-parenting environments often adopt destructive or hostile behaviors themselves.

Parental alienation is a subtle and very deceptive form of child abuse because it is often carried out through psychological and emotional manipulation. The younger the children, the more vulnerable and susceptible they are, making them easier to influence.

Below are some proven ways to stop parental alienation as soon as you notice changes in your children's behavior toward you:

- Separate your relationship with your children from their other parent and focus on what is best for your children.

- Set clear boundaries during your parenting time and do not allow your ex-spouse or ex-partner to control your children while they are with you, whether through excessive phone calls or other forms of communication.

- Do not engage with the other parent or participate in this destructive dynamic.

- Do not give the other parent any opportunity to disrespect you in front of your children.

- Do not retaliate against your children's mother or father for abusive, destructive, or damaging behavior. Remember: no response is a response.

- Do not try to defend yourself to your children. Once children have been heavily manipulated, defending yourself or trying to explain or prove anything will not change their views. Your children will eventually understand the truth, so remain at peace with yourself.

- Focus on what you can control and spend quality time with your children. Find ways to strengthen your relationship and create positive experiences together.

I have observed many divorcing parents who are very resentful and use their children to take justice into their own hands. When people are hurting, they are often more focused on their own pain, and they act from that place.

I have seen many alienating parents do this with apparent satisfaction, not realizing that they are harming and damaging their own children as a result of parental alienation.

Never ignore what you sense from anyone with whom you have ended a relationship — especially when innocent children are involved. Pay close attention to the obvious signs, signals, and patterns of what they are doing to your children.

Anyone can become "somebody else" when driven by their own pain or desperation caused by an unwanted divorce or separation. Sadly, children often become the most vulnerable and innocent victims, unable to stand up or speak out for themselves.

We further victimize ourselves by ignoring the reality of what is happening, by participating in the abuse, or by allowing things to happen because we cannot speak up or stand up for ourselves.

Sometimes, we are simply blinded by our own internal pain and fail to notice what is happening around us.

DO YOU FEEL ALONE AND ISOLATED?

Choosing to be alone and isolating ourselves is a daily choice — and sometimes it becomes our daily depressant. After my second divorce, while battling severe depression, I found myself feeling utterly alone and deeply isolated.

Even with the people I know and the large family I have, I suddenly felt completely alone in a very dark place. I had completely checked out. I also know many people who live alone and struggle with depression.

When we isolate ourselves, we enter a state of stagnation because we are not engaging with the things that make us feel "alive" and connected.

When confronted with challenges or unwanted life circumstances, our first instinct is often to withdraw from others and isolate ourselves. But this is the last thing we should do, as isolation can deepen depression.

The first step is to accept that you are not okay — because pretending will never make you feel better. When we pretend, we continue to live in pain, often out of fear of being vulnerable and honest with ourselves.

Lying to ourselves literally hurts us because it is a betrayal of who we are. When someone asks how we are doing, it is healthy to admit that we are not okay.

Being vulnerable means acknowledging the real parts of ourselves, recognizing that we are human, and accepting that we have weak moments.

> Isolation is one of the most damaging behaviors we can engage in because, when we isolate ourselves, we stop growing.

Boredom, loneliness, or feeling disconnected often stems from a lack of activities, purpose, or new experiences — or from doing the same monotonous things every day until we lose interest in life altogether.

We are social creatures by nature, and the more we interact with others or stay connected in any form, the healthier and happier we become.

115

Connecting means seeking out events, people, or activities that make you feel engaged and alive. True connection comes from finding things you enjoy — activities that bring joy, excitement, or simply a sense of being fully alive.

Life is constantly moving and changing, second by second, even if we don't always notice it. Nothing in life is truly still; everything moves and evolves moment by moment.

Therefore, we must learn to flow with the ups and downs, the highs and lows, and the constant changes of everyday life, embracing the unpredictability of life and people.

None of us can hide from this reality. Life happens whether we like it or not, and we experience the consequences of what we participate in, allow, tolerate, and accept into our lives. We create the kind of life and environment in which we live.

Sometimes, feeling sorry for ourselves is what makes us feel so alone and drives us to isolate. We hope that someone will eventually notice us and rescue us from the environment we created or chose to be in. Feeling alone, lonely, or bored can even become a habit.

It is a state of mind that we choose to remain in — and the moment we stop dwelling on negative feelings and redirect our focus toward something better, we automatically begin to shift out of that state.

Sometimes, it may be necessary to change your environment entirely — moving to a new place, meeting new people, exploring new surroundings, or creating a fresh living space.

I remember when I was in the depths of my depression, staring at every corner of my small space. It was so dark and cramped that it felt like I was literally living in a box. I could not wait to move into a new, brighter, and larger place.

The moment I started taking action, my mood changed dramatically, and my vision became clearer — simply by deciding to take the first step.

Oftentimes, when we are in a dark place, isolating ourselves feels like the natural choice, as if waiting for something better to happen. But this usually only lead us deeper into darkness.

You have the power and the innate ability to choose where you want to be and how you want to experience life. Now is the time to choose a better way to live and to explore the limitless possibilities and all the good that can happen.

ARE YOU DEPENDING ON OTHER PEOPLE FOR YOUR HAPPINESS?

Depending on other people for your happiness can be a major reason you often feel depressed — especially if you frequently experience rejection, feel unwanted, or believe you are unworthy of anyone's time or attention.

I don't know any codependent person who is truly happy and content by constantly pleasing others as a way to cope. Many of us feel that our happiness can only be found outside ourselves — in the hands of other people, or in what they can give us or do for us.

This belief never truly fulfills us. Only we can create, sustain, and nurture the happiness and fulfillment we are seeking. Happiness is an emotional experience we all yearn for, and it is a mental state we must learn to choose — anytime, anywhere, and under any circumstances.

I was one of many people who used to believe that only other people could make me happy — this belief led me to attract many negative and destructive people into my life, resulting in some of the most damaging relationships.

I felt as though I could only find happiness in a romantic relationship. This was partly because I had never been alone during the first thirty-nine years of my life, and I didn't like being on my own.

> Little did I know that being alone was exactly where I needed to be — to discover true happiness and fulfillment in life.

After my second divorce, I decided never to get involved with anyone again until I knew, in my heart and soul, that I was psychologically, physically, and emotionally ready.

After a decade of being single and truly enjoying my own company, I realized that all my life I had been chasing happiness from the wrong people and for all the wrong reasons.

Now, happy being alone, I have recognized that no one else can sustain our happiness but ourselves. As I became internally healthy, I grew more lighthearted and more attuned to what truly brings me joy — whether it's being around people, spending time with friends and family, cooking alone, reading, writing, exercising, or hiking by myself.

I have reached a state of mind where it doesn't matter what I do, where I am, or whom I am with. I have learned to engage fully in life on my own and live joyfully without needing any specific reason.

When you learn to be happy alone, "feeling good" becomes your natural state of being — what I now call my "set-point." Life always brings you back there.

When happiness, joy, and lightheartedness become so ingrained, they become your "home"—where no matter what happens, you will always find your way back home. Your heart is where your home truly is.

Happiness is a state of mind that we all need to learn to cultivate and develop. Depending on other people for your happiness is a path to unhappiness and constant disappointment.

You can never control what others think, say, or do — no matter how much you try to please them in the hopes of finding your own happiness.

Entering a romantic relationship from a place of unhappiness will never make you happy. And when people sense that you are relying on them for your happiness, they often pull away and disappear from your life.

As I was healing from my codependency and people-pleasing patterns, I noticed that codependent people spend all their energy trying to please others — not because it makes them happy, but because they are seeking attention or hoping to get something in return.

This behavior often traps them in a never-ending cycle of unhappiness and discontentment. I know this because I have been there.

Relying on anything outside of ourselves — whether people, material things, success, or achievements for our happiness—often leads to greater unhappiness, discontent, and unnecessary pain and suffering.

People come and go in our lives, and nice cars, big houses, or money can only fill the void so much — they will never bring lasting fulfillment. Attaching our happiness to others often leads to a state of depression, hurt, and constant disappointment.

Learning to be happy alone is the first skill we all need to master, because, in the end, we are always with ourselves. Children grow up and build their own lives, friends move on, and family members eventually leave.

Inevitably, we will all find ourselves alone at some point. This is the natural flow of life — a force we cannot control or prevent. Therefore, learning to embrace and find joy in our own company is essential.

After my divorces from my two back-to-back twenty-year marriages, I realized that I had been contributing to my own unhappiness and discontent — wishing that both my ex-husbands were different to meet my needs and expectations.

One day, I woke up to the reality that I had to see and accept people for who they are—and let them go if they were no longer aligned with me or meeting my needs. I wanted to grow and evolve, while they were content staying where they were.

You must love your significant other for who they are, not for what they can do for you. Let them go when they want to go, because people change over time.

And when they do change toward you, it is never because of you. They are often seeking something else for themselves, and we may no longer fit into that change. Otherwise, they would stay. You should let them go freely and never take their decision personally or turn it against yourself.

Give yourself that same respect when you decide to detach from anyone who is no longer meeting your needs. Never feel guilty for choosing what is good for you, because others are simply doing the same for themselves.

The only relationship we should all master is the unconditional relationship with ourselves. True happiness can only be found within. By caring for ourselves, fulfilling our own needs, and doing the things that make us happy — without expecting anything from others — we nurture that happiness.

You already have it within you; you just need to cultivate it. Begin by doing what is good for you, what feels right and true to you, without guilt. Today is the day to start dating yourself, pampering yourself, and falling in love with life on your own — and the right people will join you along the way.

ARE YOU ENVIOUS, JEALOUS, OR CONSTANTLY COMPARING YOURSELF OR YOUR LIFE TO OTHERS?

This is a very common daily depressant that many people experience. I often observe people constantly envying others and comparing themselves and their lives to those around them — this alone can keep you feeling depressed.

After my second divorce, I hit a very low point in how I viewed myself. I was driven by extremely low self-esteem, feeling unworthy, and believing I wasn't good enough for anything — until I realized that I was my own enemy by constantly focusing on other people.

Most people I know would say that I lived a very good life and had everything I could possibly want; some even envied my life. Yet for me, nothing was ever good enough. I was always that friend who seemed to have it all — while internally feeling inadequate, insecure, dissatisfied, and always feeling empty.

But why do we do this? Why do we envy others or constantly compare ourselves to them? The real reason is that we are not happy with ourselves. We feel insecure about our appearance, believe we are not good enough, or lack the confidence to appreciate our own accomplishments.

Whether it's being financially wealthy, physically fit, married, a parent, or having a dream job, we often dismiss all the good things we already have because we are so caught up in envying others and comparing our lives or circumstances to theirs.

Nothing is more empowering than focusing on our own lives and finding ways to improve ourselves and our circumstances. The truth is that, most people are doing the same thing we are. The very people you are comparing yourself to may be comparing themselves to you.

We create our own unhappiness, discontent, and dissatisfaction by discounting our accomplishments and dismissing all the good things we already have in our lives — family and friends, a safe and comfortable home, and, most importantly, the simple fact that we are alive and breathing.

We are free to change anything about ourselves and our lives whenever we choose. Often, we fail to realize that we already have far more to appreciate and be happy about than most people.

Sometimes, we are just so bored with our own lives — doing the same things day after day, week after week, or year after year. We become stagnant, complacent, or lose sight of the real reasons and purpose for getting up each day.

If this resonates with you, it's time to create a new way to live. Set new life goals, change your environment, or adjust the dynamics of your family or romantic relationships — anything that helps you feel alive and excited again.

The root cause of unhappiness, discontent, and dissatisfaction often comes from our own insecurities about ourselves and our lives.

Focusing on other people makes us forget that we have the same abilities to create anything we want for ourselves. Now is the time to put your focus and energy into the things you want for yourself and start making them happen — without worrying about what others are doing with their own lives.

The less attention we give to things that don't matter to us, the more time, energy, and focus we have to improve ourselves and our own lives.

ARE YOU SELF-SABOTAGING OR BORED WITH YOUR LIFE?

Feeling sorry for ourselves is often the very reason we become depressed — and what keeps us depressed. It is impossible to feel good when we know we are harming ourselves or undermining the good things in our lives.

Boredom and having nothing to do beyond repetitive daily routines — such as work, unfulfilling relationships, or feeling trapped while caring for young children, elderly parents, or sick loved ones — can leave us feeling lifeless and depressed.

Lack of anything new or exciting to do, a stale or boring intimate relationship, and a draining work life — where you can't wait for the day to end — can leave you feeling stuck.

Then you get home and repeat the same tedious daily rituals. Soon, you start comparing your life to friends or others who seem to have it all.

Before you know it, you begin feeling sorry for yourself. This is one of the most common daily depressants — and because we've been doing it for years, it becomes our normal way of life. We forget that we have the power to change anything we want in our lives.

These habits and routines become so ingrained that we lose the ability to try something new or different. A boring life becomes "normal" and comfortable, so we settle for where we are — even if we're unhappy.

Self-pity, I believe, is one of the most childish and counterproductive things we can do to ourselves — whether we are aware of it or not. We cannot go against ourselves, be our own enemy, and expect others to show compassion for us.

We are the ones who must give that compassion to ourselves — especially whenever we find ourselves detached from the things that matter to us or the things that make us happy, excited, empowered, or feel alive.

A former forty-eight-year-old male client was constantly in a self-destructive state — feeling down and depressed. Every time I met with him, he spoke about wanting to end his life. At first, I was very cautious about what to say and how to respond. Even after years of knowing him and becoming friends, he continued to repeat the same statements.

Over time, I began to notice a pattern. He often expressed these thoughts as a way to gain attention and sympathy. After hearing this repeatedly for years, one day I responded honestly as a friend and said, "You've been saying this for a long time, yet you're still here. What is really going on inside you?"

He looked surprised by my response. Then he admitted that he often held onto self-pity because he felt bored with his life and feel very alone. He realized that feeling sorry for himself had become a coping mechanism.

This story is one of many honest examples showing that most of us know exactly where we stand and how we feel about our lives. Yet instead of taking responsibility and making changes, we sometimes fall into the habit of beating ourselves up by having a pity party as an escape.

It is very common to turn against ourselves when we feel alone in life. We sabotage everything good that remains, and self-pity is a major form of self-sabotage or self-destruction — a very damaging behavior.

Other self-sabotaging behaviors include procrastination, slothfulness, doing nothing all day, and self-medicating with drugs, alcohol, or overeating. Essentially, we hurt ourselves as a way to cope with whatever challenges or pain we are experiencing.

If you are honest with yourself, you can see that no matter how bad your life may seem, you are breathing, there are good things about yourself, and something is working in your life. But when you are in self-destructive mode, you fail to see these positives — and often sabotage them.

I know it's always comforting to have someone check in on us — especially when we feel alone — to cheer us up, even if only for a moment.

Unfortunately, most people we know, including our family members, are also busy with their own lives. As adults, we are often the last thing on their minds.

We are our own love, our own best friend, and our own savior. No one can save us from anything except ourselves, and no one can love us as fully as we can once we learn to love ourselves unconditionally.

We are our own strength in moments of weakness because only we truly know what is going on inside us. So, today is the day to start treating yourself better — because you need yourself the most.

ARE YOU ALL OVER THE PLACE AND FEELING LOST IN LIFE?

This is exactly where I was during the first few years of my "Journey of Change." I felt lost, helpless, and afraid. Having no sense of purpose, no clear direction, and no real reason to get up each day is one of the main reasons many people fall into depression.

Not knowing what to do with our lives often means living in a constant state of confusion — wandering aimlessly, pacing through each day, and doing things mindlessly without intention or meaning.

After years of battling depression around the clock, one day everything became clear to me. One of the main reasons I stayed depressed for so long was that I had no reason to get up or be anywhere. When my second marriage ended, I had no idea where to begin with my life.

The weight of my past and the overwhelming feeling of depression clouded my vision. For years, I couldn't see a way out of the darkness. Until one day, I began to reflect and realized there had to be a way forward — I just needed to listen more deeply to find the answers.

That day finally came when I woke up with a powerful realization: I needed to move on from the past and stop wishing everything had been different.

One insight led to another, until a clear message emerged — I needed a sense of purpose, direction, and a plan for what I wanted to do and where I wanted to go next. The moment I began to take action; I immediately felt a renewed sense of hope and possibility.

Like I once was, many people wake up every day repeating the same boring, lifeless routines — or waiting for a miracle to change their lives, only to find that nothing ever happens.

After years of waking up feeling severely depressed, helpless, and hopeless, one day I became fully aware of a powerful truth that: Life is the Journey, and Physical Death is the Destination.

That profound realization led me to a new path and a deeper understanding — that what we do between life and death becomes our life's purpose, our roadmap, and our direction until we reach the end of the journey.

If we don't have life goals or future plans, we are essentially living aimlessly because we are not aiming for anything. We end up passively waiting for life to pass by — and in doing so, we miss the deeper reasons we were born.

You were not born just to die. We were born to live, to experience life, and to grow before we eventually leave this world. Many of us misunderstand the true meaning of life.

Our life's journey is about filling the space between the day we are born and our final day on earth with meaning, purpose, and experience.

So, if you find yourself feeling lost and without direction, now is the time to discover what you truly want to do with the time you have.

The moment you gain clarity, the next step will reveal itself, and new possibilities will begin to open as you become ready to see them.

Having a life purpose means having short-term or long-term goals for the future. The daily actions and efforts you take toward achieving those goals become your life's direction.

One reason many people feel depressed is that they lack meaningful reasons or a worthy purpose to get up each day, leaving them stuck.

We wander through life feeling lost and discouraged because we don't know what we truly want or what to do with our lives. This lack of clarity and direction often leads to feelings of depression and emptiness.

Sometimes, we lose our grip on our own lives while trying to fulfill other people's expectations and meet the pressures of society. This creates a sense that we must behave a certain way or live a specific lifestyle just to "fit in."

As a result, we lose our sense of reality and forget what we truly want for ourselves and the kind of life we genuinely desire. We become so preoccupied with trying to do or copy what everyone else is doing that we lose sight of our own path.

So today, start by asking yourself the following questions:

- Do I feel lost because I don't know who I am or what I truly want in life?

- Am I lost because I am constantly trying to fulfill other people's needs or expectations of me?

- Am I lost because I have depended on others my whole life, and now that I don't have anyone to depend on, I feel completely lost and helpless?

- When was the last time I clearly knew what I wanted in life and allowed that desire to guide me every day?

- Am I lost because I am constantly trying to please others, make everyone around me happy, or solve everyone else's problems — except my own?

The moment you turn inward and acknowledge your own longings and deepest yearnings, you will recognize that you have been living your life under the control, influence, demands, or expectations of others.

When you take full responsibility for yourself, what you truly need will begin to show up — when you are ready for it. Most of us feel paralyzed, unsure of what to do when we face life's struggles or difficulties.

Until we choose to take action and make changes, change will never happen—and now is the time to discover what you truly want — based on your own truths, your desires, the kind of life you really want, and what feels right and authentic to you — regardless of what the world thinks, says, or does.

This is your life. You get to decide how you want to live it and how you choose to experience it. You are not here to simply exist—you are here to create, to grow, and to experience life.

Every choice you make shapes your path. Choose with courage. Choose with intention. And most of all, choose in a way that honors your truths.

CHAPTER 8

TRAUMA INDUCED DEPRESSION

In Chapter Seven (7), I explained that there are two types of depression: Unconscious Depression and Conscious, or "Self-Inflicted," Depression. In this chapter, I present some of the most common examples of Unconscious Depression — the "*real*" depression caused by unresolved past life traumas.

EXAMPLE OF UNCONSCIOUS (REAL) DEPRESSION

My Story:

At the age of thirty-nine, I became consciously aware of my internal state and unconscious trauma.

Growing up in a brutal and hostile environment became the root of my depression and kept me in a state of severe emotional suffering for decades. Depression caused by deep-seated trauma is not something that can be easily faked.

I had no idea that I had lived in a depressed state my entire life — until I became aware of it. Now, having experienced severe depression and healed from it, I can clearly distinguish between "consciously choosing" to be depressed and being unconsciously depressed. Feeling unconsciously depressed twenty-four-seven was my reality.

It was only after experiencing both sides — Light and Darkness, or "Healed and Wounded" — that I fully recognized I had been living in the dark, trapped in a depressive state, until I became conscious and aware of my past-life trauma.

If you have lived long enough, you have most likely experienced traumatic life events and may still be carrying those wounds — until you become aware of them, acknowledge them, and heal.

The main purpose of healing is to become conscious of our unconscious pain, suffering, and past trauma, so that we can take control of how they influence our current choices, behaviors, and life experiences.

It took me a long time to come to terms with my past and make peace with it — especially the first thirteen years of my life, when I lived in fear and hostility in my own home, surrounded by the very people who were supposed to protect me.

Only after becoming fully aware of my own pain and suffering did I begin to understand that my parents, and others who hurt or abused me in any way, were themselves victims — victims of other victims.

At some point, we must face a very painful truth: now that we know better, we are responsible for helping ourselves heal from our pasts in whatever way we choose, so that we can move forward with our lives — regardless of how things happened.

I have listed some of the most common unconscious traumas that people carry, often without even realizing they exist.

Healing is ultimately about feeling better and reclaiming your life so that you can begin again and build a new, healthy, and wholesome life.

SELF-HATRED OR BEING YOUR OWN WORST ENEMY

If you have been abused verbally, emotionally, psychologically, physically, and or sexually— especially early in life — self-hatred is one of the most common effects of abuse.

I know many survivors of abuse, and throughout my own healing journey, I recognized that self-hatred was one of the unconscious traumas I had to confront, heal, and overcome.

Why self-hatred?
When a child is abused by parents or caregivers, they often internalize the abuse and begin to see themselves as the "bad" child. They take the blame, which can eventually develop into self-hatred for being "that bad child." This belief is often reinforced by parents or caregivers who, driven by their own guilt, project blame onto the child.

The child may carry this belief of being "bad" well into adulthood — until they become aware of the underlying trauma. So, if you find yourself hating yourself, working against yourself, or disliking who you are, look back to your childhood. Recall the person who made you feel unworthy or the one who punished or abused you for being "bad."

When you become aware of these traumas, you can begin helping yourself move beyond them and transform self-hatred into self-love, self-compassion, self-forgiveness, or self-parenting. You become your own parent — learning to comfort yourself, the wounded child within you, your pain, and your unmet needs.

Denying how we truly feel about ourselves is enough to keep us deeply depressed because we end up working against ourselves. If you pause and listen to the way you speak to yourself, you may realize that the person who has been hurting you or putting you down most often has been yourself.

It took me years to face the parts of myself I disliked—many of them rooted in old beliefs my parents and others had instilled in me. Those beliefs turned me against myself, and I became my own worst enemy.

One day, I woke up with a powerful realization: how could I not feel depressed when I was constantly undermining and working against myself in so many ways? It is painful enough to hate or dislike anyone — let alone to hate or dislike ourselves.

Spending our daily energy hating ourselves is not only very depressing but also extremely damaging to our overall health and well-being.

Self-hatred often drives people to self-destructive behaviors and, at times, to be abusive or hurtful toward others — because they are reacting from a place of pain.

- We cannot expect others to love us while we hate ourselves.

- We cannot ask others to respect us while we disrespect ourselves.

- We cannot expect others to appreciate our physical appearance when we hate every part of our body.

- We cannot expect others to believe in us if we constantly doubt ourselves and our abilities.

- We cannot spend our daily energy hating ourselves or disliking everything about ourselves and still expect to wake up each day feeling good about who we are.

- We cannot expect anyone to see us differently than how we see ourselves.

So, before you go to bed tonight, take a moment to reflect and look inward. Identify the reasons you feel the way you do about yourself.

Much of our pain and suffering comes from what we quietly or secretly hold inside. Self-parenting, self-love, self-compassion, and self-forgiveness are the keys to healing emotional pain and discomfort.

Shift your focus toward getting better and begin treating yourself a little more kindlier each day — no matter how small the progress may seem. Over time, this will place you in a healthier emotional space.

If you do not begin treating yourself better today, you may wake up tomorrow with the same painful feelings, including self-hatred. Daily self-care should always be a priority before attending to everyone else.

When we feel good about ourselves, life becomes more effortless. And when we learn to love ourselves, we no longer feel the need to seek love from others.

ARE YOU ALWAYS FEELING NERVOUS, ANXIOUS, OR AFRAID?

Having experienced severe Complex Post-Traumatic Stress Disorder (CPTSD), I struggled with constant fear, worry, generalized anxiety, nervous habits, agoraphobia, Obsessive Compulsive Disorder, restlessness, panic, and paranoia.

Those were my daily inner battles — constantly and simultaneously playing tricks on my mind — until I recognized them, brought the memories of those traumas into conscious awareness, and finally faced them.

This process also led me to discover another type of fear that I did not even know existed. Before I understood fear at all, I discovered that there are two types of fear.

TRAUMA FEARS: This type of fear is often accompanied by other symptoms, as I experienced, such as; **generalized anxiety**, CPTSD, **agoraphobia**, **nervous habits**, **paranoia**, and other fear-related conditions. Trauma fears remain active within you and can be triggered by similar events — until you become aware of them.

Once you become aware of the underlying trauma behind these fears, you gain the ability to regulate your reactions and take control of your responses when you are triggered.

INNATE OR BUILT-IN FEARS: This type of fear is a survival mechanism — a built-in protection designed to keep us safe, alive, and functioning. It activates automatically in a split second when we face danger, feel uncertain or uncomfortable, or encounter something new and unfamiliar.

We can usually recover quickly and naturally from this type of fear once the event is over, although the speed of recovery depends on the severity of the event and how it affected us.

You can learn to differentiate whether your fears stem from trauma or from a natural survival response once you become aware of both. In my experience, when I became conscious of my unconscious traumas, I noticed that intense anxiety and tremors were my automatic reactions, whenever I was triggered by a similar person or situation.

Feeling paralyzed or physically immobilized is how I automatically respond to anything new, frightening, or unfamiliar.

TRAUMA FEARS: Many people live in a state of fear caused by past traumas. Trauma fears can feel as if you are constantly haunted by traumatic memories, putting you into a fearful state — sometimes unconsciously and at times uncontrollably.

In some cases, our fears also arise from an overactive imagination, created obsessively in our minds and often fueled by delusions or paranoia as part of our survival mechanisms while growing up.

I recognized that we frequently generate our own fearful reactions through imagination, visualizing the worst possible outcomes whenever we are triggered.

In my case, Negative Thinking Addiction was something I developed as part of my coping mechanism — constantly imagining every fearful and terrifying scenario that could happen to me or worrying about what my father might do.

As one of my favorite American motivational authors, **Louise Hay**, said: "**Stop terrorizing yourself with your own thoughts**." We are often the ones terrorizing ourselves through poor thinking habits and patterns. And most of what we imagine, fear, or worry about never actually happens.

> Poor or destructive thinking habits are learned and developed as a way to survive and protect ourselves.

Before I became aware of my past traumas, I often found myself reacting uncontrollably to almost anything, because I had been traumatized by living in a horrifying home environment twenty-four-seven.

My fearful reactions often left me feeling completely paralyzed — crawling into bed became my automatic response every time I was triggered. Staying home, safe and protected, became my way of coping with fear, worry, and anxiety.

This state could last for weeks, as it mirrored what I had done as a child — hiding from my father whenever I felt terrified. As I healed and became more aware of my childhood traumas, I gradually learned to control my anxiety and manage my fearful reactions whenever I was triggered.

INNATE FEARS: After battling my own fears — or my "inner demons," which constantly tried to scare me and stop me from doing anything I wanted — I finally recognized it and came face to face with it. Innate fear is our internal, automatic reaction to any fearful thought or to encountering something that physically frightens us.

Innate fear is like a "knee-jerk reaction" designed to protect us — it serves as our survival mechanism. This fear is a natural part of being alive and will never disappear as long as we live. As **Susan Jeffers** famously wrote in her book: **Feel the Fear and Do It Anyway** – because innate fear is always within us, no matter how much we try to hide from it or run away.

We don't need to amplify our fear by dwelling on it, turning ourselves into our own source of terror. We keep running from something we can never truly escape because it is an inherent part of us.

Every person reacts to fear differently. Some respond with depression, while others may shake or twitch physically, developing nervous habits. Some run, hide, freeze, or even attack. Others experience hot flashes, start sweating, or turn to food or addictions for comfort.

Feeling fearful often comes down to a basic instinct: the fear of dying or the desire to avoid the discomfort of unwanted, unpleasant, or challenging life experiences — both good and bad.

For example: worrying about money usually stems from a fear of becoming homeless or experiencing the discomfort of hunger, which feels like a threat to survival.

Riding a roller coaster can evoke a mix of fear and excitement simultaneously.

Worrying about our children can trigger fear because we dread that something might happen to them or that they might "die." The thought of enduring the agony of emotional pain from losing someone terrifies us.

I had many profound experiences facing my own fears when I began to recognize why I was always afraid — afraid of just about anything I could imagine. This eventually led me to a major realization: the reason I was constantly fearful was that I was afraid of feeling the discomfort of being hurt — or even the discomfort of being too excited.

After years of confronting and understanding my fears, I realized that life is fundamentally about living and dying.

To truly live, we must be willing to endure all the pain and discomfort that comes with being alive — experiences that can sometimes feel like death.

I learned to embrace the fact that fears will always be part of my life, and I learned to move through my fearful reactions regardless of how I feel.

PAIN, EXCITEMENT, AND MORTALITY

You need to feel excitement in order to fully experience life. You need to feel pain and discomfort to grow, and ultimately, to come to terms with the fact that your life will eventually end. Mortality is the one certainty in life, yet we rarely speak of it openly enough to let it change the way we live.

Embracing the discomforts of daily life and accepting my own mortality made me realize that I must live each day to the fullest — despite fear. Do I want to die or get hurt? No! I don't know a single human being — even the most enlightened — who genuinely wishes to be hurt or to die.

Highly enlightened and many successful people have simply learned to face and accept their own mortality as an inevitable part of life. They have learned to act despite fear, embracing the uncomfortable or painful process as a necessary part of growth and achieving success in whatever they desire.

In other words, there is no way out — there is no cure for fear. We must learn to recognize our triggers and the root causes of our fears, and work with them. We can make our fears our allies, having them work with us and for us rather than against us.

Knowing that fear is an innate part of being alive, we must learn how to live with it. Understanding how you react to any fearful situation is the first step toward mastering it, so you can manage your responses whenever you are triggered.

By recognizing your triggers and the roots of your fears, you gain the ability to control your reactions, allowing fear to work for you rather than against you.

ARE YOU BATTLING ONE OR MORE TYPES OF ADDICTIONS?

Every addict I know has suffered complex trauma. Their addiction is often a way of coping with unconscious pain and suffering. Addiction is an unconscious habit and is frequently tied to survival mechanisms.

If your addiction has reached a point where it controls you and affects every part of your life, this constant battle can keep you feeling always depressed — battling against yourself.

Addictions are often driven by feelings of emptiness or incompleteness, which push us to seek anything that might fill the void. Unfortunately, self-destruction can become a default way to soothe our pain and discomfort.

We then become addicted to that instant relief. We keep chasing those fleeting feelings, and the cycle continues — until we become aware of it, choose another path, and commit to healthier, more conscious choices.

I call every addiction the "Momentary Impulse of Irrationality." Addiction to anything is a way of self-medicating or self-numbing, and the comedown from what you are addicted to is what keeps you feeling depressed.

Every addict I know is deeply depressed because they are hurting internally. All types of addiction are often a manifestation — or an outward expression — of something missing within us that we long for or crave. You will never truly understand what it is if you keep running from it or ignoring it.

There is a part of yourself that feels so empty, driving you to pursue things to fill the void — only you can recognize it.

I recognized my first addiction when I became helpless and powerless — codependent on an addict. I realized that my own addiction to please others, or my compulsion to try to save people from their own addictions, was really a way to fulfill my own need to be saved. And yes, people-pleasing and codependency are significant forms of addiction and self-destruction.

Later, when I began my healing journey, I recognized my severe addiction to hoarding, buying, or compulsive shipping — aimlessly collecting all kinds of "stuff" I never truly needed.

It became so consuming that it occupied me twenty-four-seven. The instant relief I felt when I bought something gave me a temporary sense of comfort and security.

After years of confronting my unconscious, destructive, and uncontrollable hoarding and buying behaviors, I was able to bring their root causes to the surface and become fully aware of them. These are the insights I discovered about my codependency, people-pleasing, and hoarding addictions:

They were deeply ingrained psychological and mental habits that I developed as part of my survival mechanism — my way of coping with pain, difficulty, and uncomfortable life situations. Both people-pleasing and hoarding gave me *"instant relief"* and a sense of comfort and security, even though they were ultimately harming me.

During my childhood, pain and self-destructive patterns came to feel like my only sense of safety and comfort. I was constantly battling myself psychologically because I had nowhere else to express myself or ask for help. I was trapped in my home, feeling helpless while being hurt and tormented by my father.

I spent the first thirty-nine years of my life surrounded by addicts and abusive, destructive people — among family members, close friends, and life partners.

These included pornography addiction, gambling, drugs, alcohol, people-pleasing, controlling behavior, attention-seeking, addiction to power, and sugar and food addictions.

I watched my loved ones struggle with their own addictions, and one of those people was my father. I learned that the only way to win this battle is through honesty and a willingness to change — not by ignoring your behavior. Until you are ready, no one else can save you, because we are ultimately our own saviors.

We all have the power to break these self-harming habits. Do not continue to inflict pain and suffering on yourself, or wage war within yourself — our enemies are within, not out there. We just need to recognize who or what they are.

A client of mine who was battling multiple addictions would always respond the same way whenever I told him he had a choice in how to act when he felt the urge: "It's easy for you to say that."

My response was: whether you realize it or not, you are conscious enough to know what you are doing before you reach that moment. You are conscious enough to stop yourself before you give in to the urge. Because one of the main causes of addiction is often a lack of self-control — or a lack of conscious effort to intervene.

If you give yourself enough time to stay sober and away from whatever you are addicted to, and take the time to observe your behavior, you will uncover many of the underlying reasons driving you to chase those things. The answers are inside you.

Nothing and no one outside of us forces us to act destructively. The driving forces behind our destructive habits always come from our desire to feel better — something only we can recognize.

Beneath every addiction is pain. As humans, we naturally dislike feeling uncomfortable or experiencing emotional distress, so we run from it. Addiction provides instant relief, allowing us to feel better temporarily. This self-destructive pattern continues until we become aware of what drives it and make the conscious decision to end it.

Addiction consumes every bit of the good in us and turns us into the person we don't want to be. Giving in to that "Momentary Impulse of Irrationality" is always the easy way out because we are often afraid to feel any discomforts. We don't want to face the parts of ourselves that we dislike or are ashamed of.

A major factor in addiction is a lack of self-control or willpower. So, next time you feel that "urge," remember you have enough time to make the right choice before you act on it. You feel the trigger before you act, and you can choose differently.

- You are aware and conscious enough to stop yourself before you reach that moment, every time you feel the craving.

- You are aware and conscious enough to turn away before going to meet friends who might tempt you.

- You are aware and conscious enough to choose a different path the moment you notice yourself heading in the wrong direction.

Just like depression, addiction is our own battle—one that only we can conquer. No one can save us from it except ourselves. You don't have to quit cold turkey. Your will to change, your desire to improve, and your conscious effort will guide you through the process. Gradual weaning works for most addicts I know.

This approach doesn't necessarily stop the urge completely or suddenly. Instead, it involves spacing out urges and replacing them with healthier activities—or simply doing nothing—until the urge eventually passes on its own.

Addiction is nothing more than an impulse: a feeling of emptiness longing to be instantly filled. Like all impulses, it fades quickly if we do not act on it.

According to **Joan Rosenberg**, PhD, creator of Emotional Mastery:

It only takes ninety (90) seconds for uncomfortable feelings to leave the body.

If we can master the ability to feel those urges and wait at least ninety seconds, chances are we can stop hurting ourselves. With conscious and deliberate effort, this practice can eventually help us overcome our addictions.

Another way to manage addiction is through exercise, because physical activity provides an instant rush that helps us feel better. The next time you feel the urge, go for a run outside, hit the gym, or swim some laps.

Every time you resist the urge, you gain more control over it—and before long, you become more in control of everything happening inside you.

The opposite is also true: every time you give in to the urge, you lose self-control and weaken your willpower. The more you give in, the weaker you become.

I know that the roots of all types of addiction can be much deeper and more complicated than simply trying to overcome them. However, any healing or recovery always begins with our willingness to do what it takes—to help ourselves recover and move past these patterns.

You have the ability and the capacity to exercise your willpower over anything. It starts with becoming aware of your behaviors and acknowledging the repetitive patterns that are controlling you. Now is the time to say **NO** to them and **YES** to yourself.

ARE YOU CARRYING A LOT OF ANGER AND RESENTMENT?

Resentment stems from suppressed, repressed, unexpressed, and unresolved negative emotions that we endure and accumulate over the years.

It is often caused by painful life experiences and by people who have abused or hurt us. Living in this emotional state is, in essence, living a deeply depressed life for as long as you hold on to this damaging emotion.

Growing up, I was not allowed to make any noise, speak a word, or express myself. As a result, I learned to suppress years of accumulated hurt, anger, and frustration—ultimately developing intense inner rage.

I remember when my father would hurt me with anything he could grab, between the ages of four and seven. I was not allowed to shed tears or show any sign of being hurt—or I would be punished even more.

I developed extraordinarily strong internal control, holding myself upright while enduring the pain of being beaten. I remember tears running down my face without blinking, terrified that my father would see me cry.

Repressed, suppressed, and unexpressed anger is one of the most common—and powerful emotions people are often unaware of, yet it is frequently the root cause of their internal pain and suffering.

My experience was unique to me, but I know that many people have lost their voices—the ability to speak up or stand up for themselves—just as I did.

You may be one of many who were constantly shunned, ignored, or rejected each time you tried to express how you felt. Over time, you may have suppressed those emotions, which can lead to anger, a sense of being out of control, and deep resentment as a way of expressing what was never allowed to be spoken.

Suppressed negative emotions can affect our overall well-being, and this alone can keep us in a state of depression—until we become aware of them and release them through healing.

If you find yourself becoming easily angry, irritated, agitated, or frustrated, losing your temper frequently—or living in constant reaction, like a time bomb ready to explode—you are most likely carrying years of suppressed negative emotions, including emotional and psychological trauma. These unconscious traumas can drive you to react uncontrollably, aggressively, and sometimes even violently.

Much of our behavior is influenced by past traumas we are not aware of. We can bring them to the surface by becoming more conscious and noticing how quickly we react to situations.

Current events often trigger these traumas, activating the unconscious parts of ourselves. One effective strategy is to pause the moment you feel the urge to react—allowing the feeling to pass on its own. Each time you do this, you become more aware and gain greater control over the things that trigger you.

Being self-aware and conscious of your moment-to-moment actions and behaviors will help you recognize your unconscious traumas and develop the ability to control yourself.

Paying close attention to how you feel and how you react to what is happening inside and around you will help you notice when you are reacting automatically or unconsciously.

The more you practice observing your reactions, the more self-aware you become—which allows you to respond with control rather than react impulsively. The more you practice self-control, the more conscious you become.

I used to call that raging feeling of anger or frustration my "Inner Dragon." Every time I felt the sensation rising in my body—like I was about to snap or attack—I would tell that feeling, "Stay there."

After years of conscious practice, all negative emotions—especially anger, anxiety, and frustration—became my best friends. Just not my favorite kind of friends, of course.

Once you learn how to process the full range of emotions in a healthy way—without reacting impulsively—you can truly experience what it feels like to be fully alive and fully human. You can express negative emotions, especially anger, without being controlled by them.

One healthy way to express anger is to acknowledge that you are angry and notice how it feels in your body. Then, respond to your feelings calmly and assertively.

ARE YOU IN A CODEPENDENT RELATIONSHIP WITH AN ADDICT OR AN ABUSIVE PARTNER?

The psychological and emotional impact of being in a codependent relationship is enough to keep you in a state of deep depression. The longer you remain in it, the more damage is done to both you and the other person.

As you may already know, severe alcohol addiction and codependency were the primary relationship dynamics I experienced growing up. My father was a violent, hostile, and abusive alcoholic, while my mother was a helpless and powerless codependent.

Our home was my nightly terror, filled with chaos and fear caused by destruction and my father's violent behavior. I watched my mother constantly trying to save him from his alcohol addiction and self-destructive behaviors.

As the oldest child, I physically experienced the agony of my parents' relationship dynamics. Later, I recreated that same environment in my own relationships—sometimes in ways that were even worse.

When I began to awaken from my severe codependency trauma, vivid flashbacks and memories resurfaced, revealing both my parents' reality and the dynamics of my second marriage.

I came to recognize that trying to help, save, or fix someone in their internal battles and struggles is like trying to take their pain away from them.

When we ourselves are broken and grappling with our own pain, we are neither strong nor self-aware enough to understand that we can never save anyone from their suffering—not even our own children.

> We cannot help anyone if we do not have the resources or
> the capacity to help ourselves.

People who struggle with addiction are often abusive in many forms—verbal, emotional, psychological, physical, and sexual—because of the unresolved pain and turmoil they carry within themselves.

And because we are dependent on them, we often tolerate the abuse. We allow them to hurt us, and we accept it. In doing so, they may begin to see us as helpless, powerless, and vulnerable.

This is how we present ourselves to them: as someone willing to be hurt and mistreated, whether we are aware of it or not. The harder you try to save someone, the worse their behavior may become—and the more destructive or abusive they can grow.

This happens because, by allowing and tolerating their behavior, we are, in effect, giving them permission to continue.

Being codependent means losing our vision of ourselves as individuals and our power to stand on our own. We lose the ability to walk away from situations that are hurting us. Codependency can also manifest as:

- Losing our sense of self-control—our ability to manage our own emotions and respond independently to life and our own needs.

- Doing things, we don't want to do to please others, even if it means hurting or displeasing ourselves.

- Being dependent on others, allowing them to make all the decisions for us. We rely on them for our entire lives, including our own happiness and internal needs. This dependence can lead to depression, leaving us feeling completely helpless and powerless.

To break free from this relationship dynamic, we must take full responsibility for ourselves and learn to make our own choices and decisions, while allowing others to live their own lives and face the consequences of their actions.

Trying to save or join anyone in their destruction only creates destruction for ourselves, because we can never truly save anyone from anything.

Codependency feels like being attached to another person's pain, driven by our own. Attempting to save someone from their suffering often stems from an unconscious desire to be saved from our own. I witnessed this in my mother growing up, and I recognized it in my own journey of codependency.

Our own pain and suffering drive us to try to save others. Until we become conscious of our own suffering, we keep repeating the same choices and behaviors—and often pass them on to our children.

When I recognized my own behavior as a helpless and powerless codependent, I realized that I was essentially reenacting my mother's codependency in my own life.

The reason people continue to abuse us or engage in destructive behavior is that we are, in part, co-creating and supporting it—by being there for them, being available to them, tolerating their behavior, or even participating in the destruction or abuse.

- The pain and suffering of others don't need to become your own.

- You don't need to be part of anything you don't want to be in.

- You don't have to participate in any activity that you know is hurting you.

- You don't need to endure the pain caused by anyone's poor choices or harmful behavior.

- You do not need to say yes to anyone just to please them, especially at the expense of hurting yourself.

After years of living in destruction in my second marriage, it was only when I became physically injured that I finally recognized the reason I ended up in that situation: I had chosen to stay, tolerate, and at times even participate in my ex-husband's behavior.

The moment I realized and accepted this truth, I dropped to my knees and asked for help. I knew this was the moment I was ready to leave for good. I was willing to do whatever it took to never go back and never look back. But it took everything in me to reach that point.

I had nothing left to give and nothing left to fight for. I was physically drained and utterly exhausted. Every part of me was ready to leave—and willing to do whatever it took to finally get out.

Oftentimes, when we see no way out of a circumstance, we have to create our own path—finding the courage to jump into the unknown, take radical action, or disrupt everything.

The moment I took that leap, hope, freedom, and liberation followed. It was as if something unbearably heavy lifted from my body, and suddenly I felt like I was going to be okay. Everything in me began to shift immediately.

> Change happens the moment you consciously and willingly detach yourself from a harmful relationship and start working on yourself.

Discover the roots and real reasons why you have been trying to save someone, because our behavior toward others is often an outward expression of what is going on inside us.

Never worry—because that person is not going anywhere if they continue doing what they are doing. You will always know where they are and how to find them.

Until they decide to change, they remain bound. Your job is to get yourself out of that life, start taking care of yourself, and begin healing the roots of your codependency.

Never try to save or fix anyone or solve anyone's problems. We can never help someone who believes there is nothing wrong with them, and no one can save us from our own struggles.

One of my favorite books on codependency, **The Dance of Wounded Souls** by **Robert Burney**: resonated deeply with me and the agonizing patterns of codependent relationships.

> Codependency really means trying to fix someone else's brokenness in the hope that they will fix us or save us from our own struggles.

Now is the time to detach, save yourself from this damaging relationship dynamic, and begin your journey toward a better, happier, more peaceful life, and fulfilling relationship.

DO YOU HAVE LOW SELF-ESTEEM OR SELF-IMAGE ISSUES?

Dealing with low self-esteem, insecurities, poor self-image, or a negative view of ourselves often stems from past traumas and the ways people in our lives made us feel. These experiences can leave us feeling depressed and constantly trying to prove to the world that we are not "less than."

Constantly trying to meet the expectations of others—or of society—about how we should look, act, or behave is a never-ending battle within ourselves. The trust is: we will never feel good enough, sexy enough, attractive enough, smart enough, or rich enough for the wrong people.

In my healing journey, I was so consumed with trying to prove everything to the world that I couldn't understand my constant need to do so—until I recognized a profound trauma: feeling deeply inadequate as a person.

> I was my own worst critic and my own worst enemy,
> shaped by how poorly I saw myself and how I felt about
> myself overall.

As I grew healthier and became more open and willing to see reality—accepting all my flaws, insecurities, and imperfections—I was astonished to hear my friends and family speak about me. Their words were completely the opposite of how I had viewed myself.

In that moment, I understood that I had been seeing myself through the filter of trauma and the limiting beliefs rooted in my upbringing.

If you grow up around unhealthy, insecure, and destructive people like I did, you most likely develop extremely low—or even nonexistent—self-esteem and self-image, along with a host of personal insecurities.

> When we grow up hearing that we're not good enough,
> those messages can take root and shape how we see ourselves.

As young children, we absorb and agree with whatever our parents, caregivers, or others around us tell us or make us believe about ourselves. We carry that identity until we become aware of those traumas, heal from them, and develop our own sense of self.

I see this on social media, where people are constantly posting edited pictures of themselves to get attention, praise, permission, or validation—and I've had my moments of this myself.

Until I realized that people may give us an "instant fix" to feel better about ourselves, I didn't understand that the root of this behavior still lies within us—especially when no one is giving us the attention we crave.

So, what can we do to stop embarrassing ourselves by constantly seeking attention, praise, approval, or validation?

- Find the roots of why you need approval, praise, or validation from others to feel worthy or valuable as a person. Who were the people who constantly made you feel inadequate growing up?

- Practice self-care, self-compassion, unconditional self-love, and radical self-acceptance. Love and accept every part of yourself—your body, the way you think, the way you talk, the way you smile—everything about yourself, inside and out.

- Practice self-forgiveness. Forgive yourself for all your past and present mistakes. Often, self-hatred is the underlying reason we see ourselves so poorly.

- Prioritize yourself above all. Do what makes you feel good, what works for you, and what feels true to you—regardless of what others think, say, or do. Make yourself, your needs, and your happiness the most important—not the opinions of anyone else.

In my healing journey, I recognized that self-neglect, lack of self-care, and low self-confidence were some of the many reasons I felt so inadequate. I did not feel comfortable or confident in my own skin, still carrying the traumas and old beliefs about who I was and how I should be, act, and behave.

It wasn't until I turned inward and began to focus on myself—giving myself all the love, care, attention, praise, approval, and validation I needed—that I started to heal.

> How we treat ourselves, how we view ourselves, and how
> we feel about ourselves are the only things that truly
> matter.

And you know what? People do not pay as much attention to us as we think they do—because most people are seeking the same thing!

DO YOU CONSTANTLY FEEL REJECTED?

Rejection is one of the most common traumas and a frequent daily depressant that many people have experienced—or continue to experience.

Beyond the trauma of being constantly rejected by our parents or caregivers while growing up, rejection is something all of us will encounter at some point in our lives.

If you suffered trauma from being constantly rejected, as I did, you don't take it lightly when people say no to you or disapprove of you.

Growing up, the attention and approval from our parents or caregivers was what we were constantly craving. So, whenever we experience rejection now, that trauma gets triggered.

Unless you are an extraordinarily successful person or a salesperson who has learned that rejection is a natural part of success, rejection affects everyone—but it can have a lasting impact on those whose childhoods were marked by persistent rejection.

After observing many people, I recognized that most have a hard time accepting rejection, whether it's small or significant. Some take it so personally that being rejected automatically puts them into a depressive state.

This is especially true for people who cannot take "no" for an answer, or when the rejection does not meet their emotional needs to feel valued, wanted, or needed.

So, why do we feel so much emotional pain when we get rejected? Simply put, it's because we don't feel worthy or good enough. This view of ourselves often comes from our past, where we were constantly made to feel that way by our parents, caregivers, or life partners. Over time, we internalized this belief: Unworthy.

If you are one of those people who cannot take rejection for any reason, always remember this: when anyone rejects you, it is simply because you don't fit what they need for themselves. Being rejected is never truly about us. Rejection only becomes personal when we turn it against ourselves.

The reality is that you could be the most capable, influential, powerful, famous, attractive, or wealthy person on earth—if you don't fit or fulfill someone's needs, you literally mean nothing to them. The truth is that what we all value most are the things or people that fulfill our needs. This is simply a fact of life.

I had a highly narcissistic client who was very conceited and arrogant—someone who always believed he could get anything he wanted, whenever he wanted it. I observed his constant efforts to impress people, only to be repeatedly rejected—and inevitably embarrass himself.

Because of his overconfidence and arrogance, he would try every possible way to compensate for one rejection after another—until he literally fell flat on his face from embarrassment and disappointment. I call this "Self-inflicted Rejection."

I noticed that his attempts to impress others were a way to feel important or simply to get attention. His destructive behavior was the source of his constant pain and suffering, often leaving him feeling low and depressed every time he was rejected. This is a clear sign that he carried unresolved trauma from past rejections.

So, the next time you feel down or depressed because of rejection, ask yourself: Why do I need to feel accepted, valued, or worthy? Why do I seek attention, validation, or try to control others to agree with me? Very often, we seek these things to fill a void within ourselves—a void only we can truly fulfill.

Sometimes, the emotional impact of rejection is a direct reflection of how we view and value ourselves. When we are secure in who we are and confident in our abilities, we don't need anything outside of ourselves to feel enough or to feel good about who we are.

So, moving forward, every time you experience rejection, it is an opportunity to check in with yourself—how you have been treating yourself and how you truly feel about yourself. The answers are always within. They lie in the kind of relationship we have with ourselves.

DO YOU ALWAYS FEEL POOR OR LIKE YOU ARE LIVING IN POVERTY?

This book is all about trauma—and scarcity or a poverty mentality is another deeply ingrained trauma or belief that many of us learned growing up. Until we teach ourselves new beliefs about money, we will continue to live in lack and scarcity.

Being and feeling poor is never just about not having money. It is about the attached traumas we endured and the lessons we learned about money growing up that keep us trapped in this internal and external state.

Beyond our limiting beliefs or mentalities about money, welcome to the modern world, where nearly everything in our lives is measured by what we have accomplished financially or materially. Along the way, we've forgotten the real reasons why we are even here on this earth.

Being born in a poor country, where the majority of the population struggles daily just to survive, we were always known as the family who "had it all." We lived the life of the "one-day millionaire" family—every time my parents received money, it would disappear in a single day because of the scarcity mentality.

In reality, we were no different from most people, living under constant fear, scarcity, and survival pressures. I adopted that same mentality about money and unconsciously recreated the same life dynamic in my two marriages: one full-time homemaker and one full-time breadwinner.

After two failed marriages, I realized how miserable I was being a homemaker. A big part of me was constantly screaming to do more than just stay home, cook, clean, and raise children.

As a woman, being a homemaker and full-time stay-at-home mother was the only role I knew for women growing up—not that there is anything wrong with that. It's about how we feel regarding the roles we play in relationships or in society.

My mother, a full-time housewife, mother, and caregiver to many, and found her value, importance, and life purpose in that role—and she still performs it passionately to this day. I, however, realized that I had unconsciously recreated another life dynamic for myself from that same trauma.

I came to understand that I was not my mother. Staying home all the time was not enough for me to feel happy or fulfilled. A large part of me was yearning for freedom and independence.

I spent years searching for answers as to why I was always living in fear of lack—constantly feeling like I was missing "something." Not just financial resources, but a sense of never having enough of anything I could think of. I even experienced living below the poverty level, always one wrong decision away from becoming homeless.

It wasn't until I recognized my thinking and behavioral patterns and began making gradual changes that things started to shift. I learned about money, the economy, and the real importance and value of money.

From my personal and intimate experiences about money, I can say this: if you let go of needing more than what you truly need and focus on what is really making you unhappy, I guarantee that money is not nearly as big a reason for your unhappiness or discontent as you think.

An unhappy marriage or relationship—or even a job you hate—may be the real reason for your discontent. Comparing our lives to other people's financial accomplishments, which we know nothing about, can put us in a desperate position, trying to "fit in" or catch up. This often leads to a stressful, unhappy, and unfulfilling life because we are literally living under other people's expectations.

When I started working on what was truly making me unhappy, unful-filled, and discontent, my perspective on money changed. I first looked inward to uncover the root causes—the real reasons I always felt like I was lacking something, especially money.

Everything we are unhappy about always lies within ourselves. External circumstances are direct reflections—or manifestations of what is going on inside us. Our wrong beliefs about money and how we view its value are often the root causes of poverty.

Trying to avoid or ignore the reality of our lives can put us in desperate situations, which can then lead to depression. The truth has a way of catching up with us, eventually forcing us to face it. So, the first step is to be honest with yourself.

I used to be one of billions of people who believed that money was the answer to everything. The reality is that most of the time, we chase money for all the wrong reasons.

This is also why the majority of people never seem to achieve enough to become truly financially free—and, more importantly, to feel free.

Most people want to be financially wealthy to buy material things to fill the void or empty spaces within themselves—and I was one of them.

I've also observed this in many of my clients who are very financially successful, yet remain unhappy, depressed, and miserable. Why? Because they are chasing money for the wrong reasons.

No matter how much they accomplish, they never find the fulfillment they seek, because they are using money to try to fill the gaps of what they are internally searching for to feel complete.

It wasn't until I found myself living in survival mode every day, constantly worrying about money, that I truly understood its core value and importance. The real reason achieving financial freedom matters is this: money is life's energy.

Money is what we need to survive and maintain the quality of our daily lives—providing comfortable housing, food, water, electricity, good medical care, and the protection necessary to stay safe and healthy. Of course, when we have more than we need, money can give us the freedom to experience a richer, fuller life.

Having more money than we need for ourselves also enables us to help others in need. The moment I realized this, my perspective on money completely changed—I no longer felt that I needed a lot of money to be happy. I have reached a state of mind where I wake up every day feeling joyful, grateful, and appreciative of everything life offers.

> Our wrong beliefs and mentality of lack and scarcity is why no amount of money will ever feel like enough, no matter how much we have.

So, start where you are financially and ask yourself why you are in this position, because for as long as we don't address the root of the problem, we will remain stuck in the same situation, often living in the same challenging financial conditions.

When you do the work and address the root cause of your unhappiness and discontentment, the resolution will emerge.

Sometimes, financial mismanagement can also be a root cause—spending all our money on nonsense, non-essentials, and unimportant material things. In doing so, we dig the hole for ourselves.

SUPERIORITY OR INFERIORITY COMPLEX

As humans, we are social creatures by nature. We tend to thrive in groups or communities, feeling connected to other human beings.

Feeling like an outcast—whether inferior, superior, alone, or separated from the majority—not only can be very lonely, but it can also be very depressing. These feelings can keep you trapped in cycles of isolation and sadness. These traits or beliefs are often learned, taught, or rooted in deeply embedded traumas.

I recognized at a very young age that we are all one and the same, and that we share the same longings as humans. This inner knowing gave me the freedom to explore life and the confidence to meet new people from anywhere in the world. I was always the friend with a diverse circle—multiracial and multicultural—welcoming connections across boundaries.

Growing up in a country where I rarely saw people of other races, racism had never existed in my world—I had never even heard the word "racism." That changed when I married someone who, blatantly but unconsciously, treated me and my family like poor, dirty aliens from another planet.

Yet I also knew that he cared for and loved us. I wanted to understand why. I observed his behavior and sought to uncover why he felt so superior and seemed so opposed to other races.

What I discovered was revealing: feeling superior, inferior, outcast, or separated from others is nothing more than a personal belief—a state of mind, or an old idea instilled in us. It's the belief that we are fundamentally different from one another, almost like different species.

Every time we are outside our familiar or comfortable environment, we can feel lost. We feel afraid, unsafe, threatened, or like outcasts—alone and vulnerable.

We now live in a world where we often feel divided from other human beings, even though we all share the same yearnings. What you want is exactly what the rest of humanity wants for themselves: a deep sense of connection, belonging, and the security of knowing that we matter.

The moment we label ourselves or others by color, status, social level, or religion, we create separation. We automatically limit ourselves, believing we belong only to these labels and the restrictions we have imposed on ourselves.

We separate ourselves, create inner conflict, and imprison ourselves with the limitations we impose. It is the way we define ourselves and others that creates this separation.

A good example is some people I know who relocated to another country where they did not speak the language. The first thing they did was seek out people from their home country, because it felt safer and gave them a sense of belonging. In doing so, they placed themselves back into a familiar environment rather than adapting to the new, exciting surroundings and creating a new culture for themselves.

They avoid feeling like strangers or being separated by staying close to others they already know, rather than embracing unfamiliar people and experiences.

The feeling of being separated, and the belief that we must belong to a specific culture or group, is something we grow up believing. True happiness and freedom come when we open ourselves to new possibilities and embrace something different.

To live fully is to have an open heart and mind—being willing to learn something new, meet different people, and experience new cultures and life experiences. We are the only ones who impose limitations on ourselves, whether we are aware of it or not.

The moment you recognize every person as yourself, or see that we are all one by nature, you begin to see yourself as a citizen of the universe—someone who perceives no boundaries or divisions between human beings.

Whenever you find yourself feeling superior, inferior, like an outcast, or separated from the world, pay attention to your self-talk, your old beliefs, and the stories you tell yourself that create those feelings.

We create our own boundaries and personal limitations. Our realities are shaped by our judgments, views, beliefs, perceptions, interpretations, and the meanings we assign to everything.

ARE YOU AFRAID TO BE ALONE OR OF BEING ALONE?

Feeling abandoned, neglected, and utterly alone during my childhood was a painful trauma that I eventually had to confront and heal from. I realized that each time someone left, my trauma of abandonment was triggered.

It could be a friend, a neighbor, or a family member visiting for just a few hours. While they were at my place, I often felt a strong sense of anxiety and loneliness, unable to understand why. Then my memories of being left alone at home by my parents would come flooding back.

As I was writing this book, a friend of mine was going through a divorce. When I told her that she was going to be okay, the first thing she said was, "I am afraid to be alone."

Like many people, the reason they remain in a state of depression is that they haven't yet learned how to live alone. The thought of being on their own terrifies them.

This is also why many people end up in unhealthy relationships. They would rather be with someone they don't truly care about than be by themselves—even if that means tolerating a person or situation that is harmful, damaging, or depressing.

Anything in our lives that we keep running away from—especially our fear of being alone—means we are running away from ourselves.

Just like the title of **Jon Kabat-Zinn**'s book; **Wherever You Go, There You Are**. We can never escape ourselves, because the reality of what we are going through will never leave us.

The more we ignore it, the more that denial can turn into self-destructive behaviors or some form of addiction as a way to cope. It's easier to run away and deny reality, especially when it's too painful or frightening to confront.

Yet the effects of avoidance stay with us everywhere we go and in everything we do. It's impossible to keep pretending that something doesn't exist while continuing to feel its discomfort or presence.

We will all end up alone at some point, facing ourselves. The fear of being alone will never disappear until you accept it as a fact of life and learn to enjoy your own company.

> By learning to enjoy life and cope with its daily challenges
> on your own, you build inner strength that will ultimate-
> ly help you thrive.

I know that learning to be your own best friend, ally, comforter, or motivator requires a great deal of internal courage. Especially if you have never been alone or haven't done things independently, it can feel terrifying. It is completely normal to feel this way at the beginning.

In the darkness of my depression, I found myself feeling very alone, lonely, and isolated. Through the agonizing experience of severe depression and feeling physically paralyzed, I had no choice but to confront every part of myself.

Little did I know that this was where I would find all the answers I had been searching for—and running away from all my life: Myself.

When I finally reached a point where I began to enjoy being alone and loving my own company, I realized that I had spent my entire life looking for answers in all the wrong people, situations, places, events, and environments.

I spent my entire life running away from myself—the good, the bad, and the ugly. It took many years of quiet and alone time to accept every part of me, especially my past. These were parts of me I had to confront, accept, and come to terms with.

Only then could I stop running from my own shadow and be free—to truly enjoy life on my own. The fear of being alone is much like the fear of our own shadow.

After years of spending time alone, I eventually found that I no longer enjoyed crowded, noisy places. I had grown accustomed to the tranquility and peace of being alone, of doing things on my own.

Had I not spent enough time alone with myself, I would still be chasing the wrong people, the wrong places, and the wrong environments—trying to run away from myself.

I have also seen so many people return to destructive and unhappy relationships shortly after a breakup, simply because they couldn't handle being alone with themselves.

Stop scaring yourself and stop running from yourself. Everything you need is within you—it is not out there, not in anyone else, and not in anything external. You just need to sit with yourself long enough, embrace your everyday life, and do things on your own.

Be careful, though—because as you begin to love your own company, you may discover that you can become your own love, your own best friend, and may not need anyone else to be happy at all!

Today, is the day to start learning how to enjoy your own company, because you need yourself the most.

DO YOU FEEL VICTIMIZED, HELPLESS, AND POWER-LESS?

A victim mentality—and the accompanying feelings of helplessness and powerlessness—are ingrained beliefs and destructive habits that many of us develop over time.

Growing up, we were often not taught personal responsibility or given enough opportunities to take responsibility for ourselves. As a result, we never truly learned how to do so.

In the early stages of my healing, when I began journaling about my feelings, all I could write were the names of people I blamed for everything that had happened—and was still happening in my life.

I wrote about how "They" ruined my life, how they made me feel, and how they deserved to be in my position. For the longest time, I never looked at myself or examined my own role in any of it.

One day, I realized that I was keeping myself depressed, helpless, powerless, and imprisoned—waiting for everything and everyone to come and rescue me. Because I saw myself as the "victim," I believed that others had to save me and pull me out of the black hole I had consciously and unconsciously created.

I didn't like the condition of my life, and I hated myself for the poor choices, decisions, and mistakes I had made. I didn't want to face myself or accept that I was failing in many areas of my life. Blaming everything and everyone else felt easier—and, at the time, it even felt good.

Until I finally realized that no one was ever going to come and save me, apologize to me, or feel sorry for me.

- Feeling victimized, helpless, or powerless can lead to depression, as we blame everyone or everything for what has happened—or is happening in our lives.

- We victimize ourselves by blaming others because it feels easier than taking responsibility for our own actions, choices, and decisions.

- Whether we are aware of it or not, we often attract people or life events—both wanted and unwanted—based on who we are and what we carry within us. In this way, we always play a part in whatever happens in our lives.

- Feeling helpless or powerless is a learned habit and behavior that must be unlearn and relearn once we recognize it.

- Blaming others and feeling victimized often reflects unhappiness with the outcomes we created or contributed to, so we shift the blame to others or to circumstances.

- Blaming and feeling victimized can also signal regret over unmet desires, prompting us to assign blame to everyone involved.

- A lack of responsibility can stem from entitlement—the belief that the world owes us everything we want or need. When expectations are not met, we feel victimized, betrayed, or deceived.

After years of healing and gaining clarity, I recognized that life is an individual journey. Mastering ourselves and our own lives is the first moral obligation we must fulfill—for ourselves—because only we can achieve our own sense of fulfillment.

It all begins by taking full responsibility for every area of our lives.

ARE YOU A CONTROLLING OR PERFECTIONISTIC?

Most people I know who are controlling are also perfectionistic—because perfectionism is, in many ways, a form of control. Can this contribute to depression? Absolutely.

When these habits or behaviors become disordered or destructive, they can consume you. Being consumed by the need to control or perfect everything you can think of is one of the most toxic and energy-draining patterns we can impose on ourselves.

Growing up with a very abusive, perfectionistic, and controlling father, I watched him become completely consumed by ordering and controlling us—so much so that it hurt all of us.

As a result, I developed perfectionistic tendencies, until I realized that trying to perfect everything in my life was my way of coping with what I was experiencing internally.

Later, I married someone with personality traits very similar to my father's, drawn in by that familiar feeling of being controlled and constantly scrutinized.

I watched both my father and my ex-husband become consumed by their own behaviors, trying to control all of us and everything they could think of.

Through my experiences with my very controlling and perfectionistic father, being married to a remarkably similar person, and observing my own perfectionistic tendencies, I discovered the differences between perfectionistic and controlling personalities:

CONTROLLING – Often try to control people.

- You are controlling if you constantly try to manage the people around you.

- You install a driving monitoring system in your children's or partner's car to control what they do and where they go.

- You put a camera in your house—not necessarily to catch intruders, but because you enjoy having the power of knowing what everyone is doing.

- You have access to your partner's or grown-up children's phones, email accounts, social media, bank accounts, or other personal and private spaces or possessions that you shouldn't be invading—because it gives you a sense of power and control over them.

- You hire a private detective to follow your spouse or partner to monitor what they are doing.

- You constantly check on your partner's whereabouts multiple times a day while at work, sometimes even setting time limits for everything they do.

PERFECTIONISTIC – Often try to control objects.

- You are perfectionistic, and sometimes perfectionism is linked to OCD (Obsessive-Compulsive Disorder). You constantly or obsessively try to perfect every object, including the appearance of people.

- You constantly try to arrange and rearrange things perfectly, yet you still cannot seem to achieve true "perfection."

- You notice every single detail in everything.

- You often focus on the outward appearances of people—for example, how perfectly they are dressed, how neat and clean they are, how well colors match, the shoes they are wearing, or how they style their hair or trim their nails.

- You often repeat the same actions over and over to perfect them, to the point of exhaustion or mental strain.

- You are frequently consumed by trying to perfect everything you focus on, from the smallest details to the largest tasks.

Growing up under my father's controlling and perfectionistic ways, I absorbed those traits myself—never realizing how deeply perfectionism was shaping and controlling my life.

It wasn't until I became aware of this and began healing from that trauma that I was able to live a balanced life—**Perfectly Imperfect**.

When we are the ones dealing with destructive habits or behaviors, we often don't see them—but others around us do. Being controlled felt very normal to me growing up.

Later, I married another very controlling person and watched him become consumed by constantly trying to control everything.

The perfectionistic person I married reflected my own perfectionism—and the unresolved trauma behind it.

So, what is really going on when we try to control or perfect everything? It gives us a sense of comfort—or power—knowing that we are in control. Controlling or perfecting everything or everyone can make us feel powerful, which provides a certain relief or sense of comfort.

Being in control of our own behavior and our own lives is one thing. But trying to control or perfect everything—and everyone—beyond a healthy point, to the extent that it becomes destructive or distorting, creates suffering for ourselves and damage to those around us. I have witnessed this firsthand in my own life.

In my healing journey, I have gained many profound insights. Beneath all types of destructive habits and behaviors lie empty emotional spaces within us, longing to be filled—whether we are aware of them or not. We often try to fill that emptiness from external sources.

This may show up as controlling people, perfecting objects, or engaging in other destructive habits. Until we become aware of how damaging these patterns are to ourselves and others, these behaviors continue to serve as sources of comfort, power, or security—a way to cope.

So, whenever you find yourself consumed by the need to control or perfect anything or anyone, pause and look inside yourself to find the real reasons driving this behavior.

Unconscious or uncontrollable habits are often physical manifestations of how we truly feel inside or where we are psychologically.

CHAPTER 9

RECOGNIZE AND STUDY YOUR UNCONSCIOUS TRAUMA

After years of studying and understanding my very personal journey through severe depression and healing my traumas, I have come to know deeply that healing is profoundly personal and intimate work—work only we can do for ourselves.

We alone can heal ourselves by being willing to do the necessary work, because no one else truly knows where our pains lie or where they come from. Healing is not a journey to forget our pain; it is about accepting our painful past and coming to terms with it.

Healing can also mean becoming aware of what is happening inside and outside of ourselves and understanding every part of who we are. Then, we must come to terms with what we discover.

When you notice yourself behaving in certain ways and feel controlled by actions you don't consciously choose, it is likely that you are reacting from unconscious trauma.

When you catch yourself feeling angry, frustrated, jealous, or out of control, instead of reacting, sit with those emotions and try to remember the person in your past who consistently triggered you to respond that way.

Was it your father? Your mother? A brother, sister, or life partner? Or were you bullied by someone at school who always made you feel that way? Then, connect that memory to your current behavior.

If you notice yourself feeling needy or seeking constant attention, try to recall your past and the person who consistently rejected you. Was it your mother, your father, or another caregiver or family member who made you feel unwanted? Then, link that experience to your current behavior.

Whenever you find yourself feeling unworthy, not good enough, small, inadequate, or incapable, allow yourself to feel those emotions while remembering the person or people from your past who consistently made you feel that way—those who made you feel like nothing you did was ever good enough.

Was it someone you had a close relationship with? Your mother, father, brother, sister, caregiver, or another family member? Then, connect that experience to your current behavior.

The examples above are just a few of the many ways you may be reacting, responding, or behaving from unconscious traumas. You can bring past trauma or painful memories to the surface by revisiting them and becoming fully aware of them.

Be prepared to experience these memories more intensely than when they originally occurred, because now you are re-experiencing them with full awareness.

This heightened awareness can make the emotions feel much stronger—and sometimes even excruciating—compared to when you first experienced them while unaware, unconscious, or only partially conscious.

When you find yourself in the same destructive environments, toxic relationships, or repeating unhealthy habits and behaviors, it is an indication that your actions are being driven unconsciously by past traumas or experiences from earlier in life.

If you notice yourself behaving like your father, mother, or any other family member, it may indicate that you are still carrying aspects of their identities—acting and reacting as they did.

I remember when I realized that I was literally reliving my past in my present life. That moment of recognition was so profound that I could not fully grasp the reality out of confusion—until I became fully aware of it.

Depression is often the surface manifestation of past traumas that remain active within us. Most people walk through life unconsciously carrying years of accumulated, suppressed, and unresolved painful experiences, which drive their unconscious and often destructive choices and behaviors.

If you look back at your life, consider the last five years: Where have you been, and what have you been doing that was destructive and made you very unhappy? Why could you not walk away from those situations, even though, deep down, you knew you were in the wrong place or with the wrong person?

This happens because, if pain and suffering are all we have ever known, being unhappy and miserable begins to feel normal.

Until you realize and recognize that there is a way out, you will never truly experience the brighter, happier side of life—or even understand what true happiness really feels like.

I'm not talking about the kind of happiness that comes from a smile or pretending to be happy. I mean the kind of happiness that comes from being internally healthy—a happiness that arises from within ourselves.

If you grew up in a very destructive environment, surrounded by abusive parents, caregivers, or other family members, you are likely still carrying the psychological and emotional impact of that environment.

As a result, you may find yourself being destructive toward yourself and others—not because you want to, but because you don't know any other way to comfort your own pain.

We often take our pain out on something—addictions, work, or other people—as a way to cope. The saying, "Hurt people, hurt people," is true, but what I know for sure is this: most hurt people don't consciously or intentionally hurt anyone.

People are often only responding or reacting from their own pain. So, if you grow up in a very painful environment and pain is all you know, pain is what you will give to others. We must first have experienced love to be able to give love and truly understand its meaning.

We can never fully relate to compassion and love if we ourselves have never experienced it and are the ones most in need of it. We simply can't give what we don't have the capacity to give.

As I become increasingly healthy, I sense wounded and hurtful people more clearly—people who constantly try to hurt themselves and others to cope. Knowing how unconscious they are of their actions, I understand that they are expressing themselves from a place of pain.

Because that is all they know, that is all that feels true for them. "Pain is their love." We are all shaped by the painful circumstances and environments in which we grew up—but that is not who we are.

How our past shaped us is not our true self or our real nature as human beings. We grow up believing many wrong things about ourselves because that is how we were made to believe we are. But deep down, inside all of us, there is truth—and it feels good and right when we find it and when we live from that place.

We simply never learned how to express our true nature, either because we were not allowed or because we were afraid to express ourselves in ways that felt natural and true to us.

Now that you know better, you can change that and get to know who you really are inside. But if you allow yourself to remain depressed all the time, you are blocking the bigger, brighter, and better side of yourself.

Focusing on the negative parts of yourself only creates more suffering because you are working against yourself. Your true nature feels authentic, it feels right, it feels freeing, and it feels good to simply be. The root of much of our suffering comes from the unconscious traumas we have endured throughout our lives.

Healing begins the moment we become conscious and fully aware of these traumas—by understanding where our pain comes from and recognizing who has hurt us. With this awareness, forgiveness becomes effortless and natural, because now you truly know and understand.

Keep helping yourself and do what you can every day, regardless of how much progress you make. Over time, you will move beyond depression and rise above it.

You will feel the changes and improvements in yourself each time you try. It is impossible not to feel better when you are doing the right things.

The miraculous healing of my severe depression and complex trauma was driven by my conviction—by following what felt true for me based on my personal experiences.

Answers often appear when things improve, even without asking for them. Confronting and accepting the truth of everything happening in our lives is the beginning of the healing process.

As I learned the traits of every person who was part of my past, as well as those still in my current life, I discovered that healing and compassion arise simply from understanding why people behave the way they do.

When you understand yourself and your true nature, that understanding naturally extends to others, because we are all fundamentally connected.

I had to revisit and relive my past life events as far back as I could remember. Memories continued to surface, often simultaneously, and it sometimes felt so overwhelming that I didn't want to remember any of it.

But I knew that revisiting my past was the only way to understand my current behaviors. My unresolved past was keeping me trapped in a state of suffering and deep depression.

Confronting my past and becoming aware of my unconscious traumas was the only way for me to stop recreating—and continuously reliving—the same destructive and very painful patterns in my life.

Depression forced me to visit the darkest parts of my past so that I could understand the part of myself that was longing to be seen and finally make peace with it all.

Only then could I truly live in peace. Every part of my wounded being was yearning for peace—a peace that could only come from being internally whole and healthy.

Had I chosen to give up, with my very distorted mentality, wounded heart, and troubled spirit, I would never have known the other side of life—the life beyond the suffering I had always known.

As I grew healthier, I began to see myself becoming a completely different person. I slowly sensed myself detaching from the old identity that had been shaped by others, reclaiming who I truly was.

As I began to see and experience changes in myself, I found myself slowly becoming the person I wanted to be—in the way I think, speak, act, and behave.

I gradually built my new identity, and you should do your best to do the same for yourself—because no one is coming to save us from life's struggles or pull us out of depression.

No one else can heal us but ourselves. It is our responsibility to help ourselves, because this is a battle only we can truly understand and navigate.

Depression is not something we can completely prevent, because there are many things in life beyond our control. Depression is—and will always be—part of our life's journey, because unexpected and unwanted events will continue to arise, whether we ask for them or not.

People will do things, and circumstances will happen that are beyond our control—this is one of the certain facts of life. Any painful life event can trigger depression because of its psychological and emotional impact. I believe that depression can come and go as part of being alive.

Unless we are healed, healthy, and conscious enough to understand what is happening inside and outside of us, the onset of depression can easily pull us back into that dark place.

You can create your own breakthrough—not only to win your personal battle with depression, but to heal yourself from the inside out. When you are free from your traumas and have addressed the roots of your depression, you will experience true freedom and live life free from suffering.

Our unconscious traumas are the driving forces behind the destructive choices we repeat, even when they harm ourselves and those around us.

The unconscious part of yourself is the one controlling your behavior. Revisiting your past and coming to terms with all your unresolved pain and suffering is the path to freedom. Our pain and suffering live within us, and only we can free ourselves from it.

By studying and understanding every part of ourselves, we take responsibility for our own lives. Our life is our work, and our needs are our own responsibility to fulfill—above all. No one else, and nothing outside of us, can sustain the fulfillment we seek.

Every day is a chance to turn your life around, and you will do it in your own way—without anyone telling you what to do or how to do it. The process may not be as easy or as fast as you wish, but your willingness, patience, and consistent effort will take you there.

Today is the day to start.

MEDICATION IS A PERSONAL CHOICE

In my personal experience, medication was never an option. By the time I recognized what was happening to me, I had already learned so much about my condition through extensive self-education—searching for every possible answer—which eventually led me to heal myself.

As I write this book, a very close family member unexpectedly entered a destructive phase in her life and was diagnosed with manic depression, being prescribed multiple types of medication.

The medications weakened her to the point that she immediately became like a zombie—walking around and going about her day aimlessly. She went from being energetic, happy, and bubbly, never seeming to have a dull moment, to noticeably quiet and slow. The medications completely controlled her.

After being on them for about two weeks, she began to resist and openly shared how she felt: numb, heavy, and visibly dragging herself through the day.

Without a second thought, we stopped giving her the large doses. In doing so, we were able to save her from the crippling effects of the medications, which could have permanently harmed her.

Based on my personal experience of choosing not to medicate the symptoms of my depression, combined with my experience with a very close family member who tried to take medications, I became even more convinced that my belief was correct: **Medication does not cure depression.**

I emerged from severe depression and healed my profound psychological traumas—completely medication-free.

"Depression is a life trauma, not a medical condition."

I am living proof that it is possible to overcome severe depression and multiple complex traumas—especially thirteen years of severe childhood abuse—without any help from prescribed medications.

Not knowing ourselves and not understanding the root causes of our psychological or emotional pain and trauma, is a major reason why many people are misdiagnosed and treated with the wrong medications—often ending up feeling worse rather than better.

Internal courage and my willingness to give myself the chance to find my own answers became my guiding light out of the very dark and agonizing experience of severe depression and severe complex psychological traumas.

I became very conscious and aware of what was happening within me, and I never doubted for a moment that I would find my own answers. At the same time, I kept an open mind to seek medical help if that moment came—if I could no longer manage it on my own. I was certain that I would know when I had reached that point.

I began my healing process by practicing CBT (Cognitive Behavioral Therapy), or what I now call Cognitive Healing—a process I describe as "rewiring my brain."

I lived very consciously, paying close attention to what was happening in my everyday life and constantly making changes, redirecting myself toward what felt good, right, and true to me.

As I started this process, I could feel the heaviness and resistance within me—fighting against myself every time I tried to focus on even a simple task. But I was determined to keep trying. Gradually, I began to sense a shift, and my thinking patterns started to change—one directed thought and conscious physical action at a time.

Cognitive Behavioral Therapy, or CBT, became my way of living—deliberately paying close attention to how my thoughts connected to my feelings, and then to my physical state, moment by moment.

After about two years of consciously practicing CBT and staying fully awake and aware during my waking hours, I began to notice subtle but meaningful changes in myself. Each small shift gave me hope and motivation to keep going.

One healing practice led to another, eventually guiding me to heal every part of my wounded being. Over time, the process of healing transformed the direction of my entire life for the better.

I know that I am not alone in this battle called depression—or, more broadly, in facing a very human condition that we are likely to experience at some point in our lives, often unexpectedly and unwillingly, whether we want it or not.

Life continues to unfold because we are all part of this ever-changing, evolving life force. Nature works on us twenty-four-seven, and none of us can control or stop these changes from happening.

Depression is simply part of being human, often arriving when we least expect it. Mastering every part of ourselves and understanding the true nature of our personal journey through depression is what can save us from being controlled—or crippled—by it.

When I finally understood my journey through depression and the reasons behind it, I became willing to do whatever it took to heal myself. I was not about to let anyone tell me what to do or how to do it—because only I truly knew what was happening inside me.

I took on the challenge of tracing every step of how I had been hurt, abused, terrorized, tortured, and traumatized. This process allowed me to understand where all my pain was coming from—the root cause of my severe depression.

Reflecting on the years of trauma I endured at the hands of my father every day for thirteen years, I can say without hesitation: healing severe psychological trauma is not an easy process.

Unless you are willing and ready to do the work—and willing to endure whatever it takes to help yourself—it can feel utterly exhausting and excruciating.

I often felt completely drained, trying to stay conscious and attentive to every bit of my mental and physical experience, fully consumed by the healing process.

After years of deliberate, conscious healing of every part of my wounded being, I became less reactive, and everything began to feel more normal and natural again. One day, I realized that I had made it through. You will recognize the profound changes within yourself when you become internally healthy.

It feels freeing. It feels empowering. It feels like love. You become more hopeful, more empathetic, and more compassionate. The aspect I noticed most about myself was a deep sense of connection—to everything, especially to people.

Healing allows you to experience the full gamut of human emotions—and by experiencing it all, you come to understand the multi-dimensional nature of being human and the very essence of humanity as a whole.

CHAPTER 10

RECOGNIZE DEPRESSION AND RISE ABOVE IT

When we face any painful or unwanted life event, our natural response is often to take it personally. It can feel as though we are the only ones dealing with hardship or failure.

The reality, however, is that most people are facing some type of life battle—whether it's depression, medical illness, divorce, the death of a loved one, financial struggles, or other painful and unwanted situations.

We often turn against ourselves, which can make us feel helpless and alone—but we are never truly alone. Life is a universal journey. Every human being is on their own path, fighting to survive or striving to create a better life.

We are all walking a path toward somewhere, on a quest for something—whatever that may be.

So, whenever you find yourself feeling lost, confused, hurt, or alone, the first step is to accept and acknowledge the life event that has brought you to that state.

Mourning a loss and feeling the pain are part of the process of acceptance—but only up to a certain point. Every painful life event needs to be fully felt, processed, and addressed. Eventually, you must accept the reality of what is happening in your life.

Then begin to help yourself slowly recover. No one else can free us from our personal struggles or emotional pain—only we can do that for ourselves.

Psychological and emotional healing can feel like a roller coaster ride. Some days may be excruciating, while on other days you may feel fully alive again. These are normal stages of healing.

You must learn to process emotional pain and embrace its intensity, experiencing the full gamut of emotions. Unwanted life events are beyond our control and cannot be prevented. Avoiding, denying, or trying to escape the pain will only prolong the healing process.

The best way to process pain is to sit with it, fully feel it, and allow it to move through you as it arises—until it eventually fades and disappears on its own. When this happens, you will emerge feeling lighter, stronger—and eventually heal.

Depression is one of the most deceptive human conditions a person can experience. It is also one of the most frequently misdiagnosed, due to its complexity and the many subtle symptoms that accompany it—symptoms that only we can truly recognize within ourselves.

I consider myself fortunate because I was able to avoid being misdiagnosed and treated with the wrong medications, which could have been debilitating. Every unwanted life event carries some level of emotional and psychological impact.

We must learn to embrace every painful emotional experience and work through the mourning process in order to recover and move forward.

At some point, you will need to decide to get up, gather yourself, and begin engaging with life again—while you still have the energy and the will to do so. Don't let yourself reach a point of despair or powerlessness and remain stuck there.

Emotional pain can easily deceive us and quickly pull us into the dark place we most want to avoid—**depression**. Healing and maintaining emotional health are our defenses against the impact of unexpected life's events.

It is very easy to feel sorry for ourselves when we feel alone in what we are going through. If you suddenly notice that everyone you know seems unavailable or unreachable, it may be because most people are dealing with struggles similar to our own.

Most people pretend that everything is fine or that they have it all figured out. The reality is that many are hiding their own pain behind a smile or the stories they tell the world as a way to cope. Most people are struggling with something we know nothing about.

It is often easier to pretend or run from our pain than to be vulnerable and admit that we are hurting. We are all responsible for our own lives and for what happens within them.

Depression is very deceptive. My experience with severe depression was subtle yet incredibly powerful, which helped me understand why so many people fail to realize they are dealing with real, clinical depression. By the time we recognize it, we are often already deeply entrenched.

When I finally recognized that I was battling severe depression, I was already extremely weak and felt physically paralyzed. The discipline of sitting still and listening to every subtle change happening inside and around me became my guiding light through that dark journey.

It is important to recognize the difference between feeling sad or depressed for part of the day and feeling sad or depressed all the time, around the clock. When you are battling real depression, your emotional state often does not change or improve, no matter what you do.

You may lose interest in everything—even in the things you once loved. They can suddenly feel tasteless and meaningless. You may feel helpless, powerless, and overwhelmed by sadness, with little to no energy. You may feel groggy or exhausted all the time, sleep excessively, or struggle to sleep at all.

Notice sudden changes in how you see the world around you and how you feel, moment by moment. Direct your awareness to everything you observe, no matter what it is.

Don't give in to the heavy feeling of exhaustion—because the more you give in, the deeper it may pull you into the darkness of depression.

It is crucial to stay conscious, recognize where you are internally, and acknowledge it so that you can actively work against it.

START SMALL AND START WHERE YOU ARE

Rumination is one of the most common symptoms of depression. Each day, the moment you open your eyes, intrusive thoughts may begin to overwhelm you—replaying and imagining unrealistic, repetitive scenarios.

Don't let yourself remain trapped in that state of delusion or paranoia. Shift your focus to change your mood: get out of bed and do whatever feels lighter or more manageable. Even if you feel you have no energy or interest, don't give in to the heaviness that tries to keep you immobilized.

> Use your willpower to move physically as much and as often as you can during your waking hours.

FIND YOUR INNER STRENGTH

Faith is trusting in the unknown and embracing uncertainty. If you don't have someone you can speak with regularly, as I once experienced—especially during the quiet hours of the night—begin by paying close attention to how you truly feel.

If you practice religion or prayer, this is the time to lean into your faith more deeply than ever. Pray as if you are speaking to someone who is truly present with you—listening and holding space for you. Express your thoughts and the parts of yourself that have long needed a voice.

You can do this whenever you feel the need to release your emotions, because years of unexpressed, suppressed, or repressed feelings must surface in order for you to heal and be free.

Face the part of yourself that you have abandoned and neglected all your life. If you were to lie down right now, close your eyes, and imagine looking at yourself, and reflect:

- What do you see in that person?

- What would you like to say to that person?

- Where have you been, and what have you been doing over the last few years that caused you to lose your grasp on life?

- How did you end up on this beaten path, and why do you feel so lost and alone at this moment?

Perhaps you have forgotten your own existence on this earth because you have been so focused on everything and everyone else around you. You forgot that the person you truly needed all this time was yourself.

Now is the time to be there for yourself—especially in your weakest moments.

FEEL YOUR BODY

Feel every sensation in your body and listen to its messages.

After years of trying and experimenting with every possible way to feel better, I realized one day that my body was resisting everything I intended to do.

This was before I understood that our thoughts, feelings, and physical actions are all connected. For meaningful change to occur, they must be aligned and work together. Without this understanding, we often rely on only one aspect—thinking, feeling, or acting—while neglecting the others.

We may intend to do something, but if our body is saying no, we often end up following its lead instead. Even what we label as "laziness" can be deeply ingrained habits or coping mechanisms developed from past trauma, automatically activated to comfort or protect ourselves.

Your journey through depression is unique and very personal. The excruciating pain of depression is something only you can truly recognize within yourself.

No matter how much you try to explain it to others, there are moments when you are left alone with that truth. This is why it is important to acknowledge your experience—and every layer of pain—so you can begin to help yourself out of that state. We must learn to identify the emotions we are experiencing to understand them.

Listen closely: Where is the pain really coming from? Does it feel like anger or resentment? Guilt? Regret? Or does it stem from feeling victimized, helpless, or hopeless—like you have lost your sense of power and agency?

When you become aware, attuned, and learn to listen to every discomfort in your body, answers will begin to appear—in glimpses of memories, ideas, or feelings of hope, freedom, or relief.

> Our journey through depression is a battle against ourselves, because no one else can understand our experience better than we can.

If you can dwell on the things that keep you feeling depressed, you can also choose to redirect your focus and dwell on what makes you feel better—every single day.

Now is the time to give yourself that chance and be there for yourself, because you owe it to yourself.

CHAPTER 11

BEFRIEND YOUR DEPRESSION

Depression is like the worst relationship you've ever had—depression is your partner. You want to understand it completely, learn from it, and eventually break up with it when you've had enough and are ready to move on.

The feeling of being severely depressed was foreign and unfamiliar to me. Yet my curiosity about what I was experiencing led me to discover parts of myself and aspects of life I hadn't realized existed.

I found my own path to healing because I was willing to understand everything. When you become open to everything, you begin to notice everything, because you are receptive and ready to receive whatever comes your way, no matter what it may be.

In my case, a current life event activated unconscious traumas, which then led to depression. I believe that any painful life event can trigger past traumas and potentially set us on a journey into depression.

So, whatever life event triggered your depression, never hold back or suppress your emotions. Cry your heart out when you feel like crying or call a friend who is willing to just listen and let you express how you feel.

Never run away from the reality of what you are going through, because doing so will only prolong your healing and recovery.

The art of healing lies in becoming comfortable with feeling the pain and learning how to process it in a healthy way—before it escalates into suffering or depression.

Never run to the wrong people or place yourself in destructive environments where alcohol, drugs, or other harmful influences are present. Running away from any unwanted life event is often our first and easiest way to avoid feeling pain or emotional discomfort.

But this usually leads to more pain and more problems to resolve. When we are not in the right state of mind, we often make poor choices, driven by the desire to feel better instantly without considering the consequences.

Dwelling on the feeling of being depressed was one of the reasons I stayed in that state longer than I needed to. We sense everything within us, so we know what we are going through.

Yet we often choose to "dwell" on the agonizing feeling of depression as a way to cope—because, over time, feeling depressed can become our comfortable state or comfort zone.

Only when we recognize that we are the ones keeping ourselves in that state can we begin to help ourselves. Acknowledging what you are going through is the first step in your healing and recovery, rather than dwelling on it or denying its existence.

Our primary responsibility when any painful life event occurs is to care for ourselves, because that is what we need most. Let others be with themselves while you focus on helping yourself.

Listen to your inner voice trying to get your attention and accept the reality of your current life situation exactly as it is—without wishing it were different. We often find answers when we turn inward and ask ourselves honest questions.

Questions provide answers. When I began asking myself empowering questions such as;

- How did I end up here?

- What was I doing without being aware of it?

- What part did I play in this situation that brought me here?

The more I asked, the more answers appeared, until one day I realized I had solved all the puzzles.

Perhaps you can start by revisiting your life, reflecting on the past ten years, and tracing the journey from today backward. You will find many answers connected to your current life situation, because things don't simply happen by chance.

Life events often arise from small, incremental situations that we have ignored or kept running away from. Most life crises or catastrophes don't come as complete surprises, even though they can feel as if they appear out of nowhere when we least expect them.

The reality is that the impact accumulates and often hits all at once, leaving us feeling overwhelmed. So, the best thing you can do is to sit with it until you gain some clarity.

Reacting out of retaliation, frustration, rage, anger, or a desire for revenge can cause more harm and create additional problems to deal with later. Let others be on their own and give them the time and space they need, while you focus on helping yourself.

Work on feeling better and getting into the right state of mind, because we often try to control everything—even the things over which we have no control.

Recall your past experiences, going all the way back to your childhood, and connect them to your life over the last ten years. Look for patterns, especially in your repetitive mistakes, poor choices, or decisions, until you find the connections throughout your life.

We are born without a sense of ourselves or of the world around us. Everything we know—or don't know—is learned and accumulated through habits, behaviors, and beliefs passed down from our parents or caregivers. Whatever was taught to us, we absorbed and accepted as facts or truths.

We often carry traits or aspects of the personalities of one or both of our parents or caregivers. This happens because we mimic and absorb what we see in others during the first seven years of our lives—until we gain self-awareness and begin to develop our own identity.

According to American developmental biologist **Dr. Bruce Lipton**:

During the first seven years of our lives, our brains are designed to "download" programs simply by observing others. Many of the behaviors we absorb during this time can be self-sabotaging and disempowering.

Every traumatic life event you experience represents a broken piece that needs to be repaired. Life traumas can also be part of a generational chain, and the only way to break free from this long chain is to understand your past and heal from it.

We are the product of our upbringing and the environments in which we were raised. Often, we go through life unaware of what is really going on inside us, which can lead to repetitive and destructive habits, mistakes, choices, and behaviors.

We often end up in the same types of destructive people and environments that we unconsciously don't want to be in. This is the "sleeping" part of ourselves that we are not yet aware of.

Until we revisit that old part of ourselves and bring it into awareness, we will continue making the same mistakes because we are responding and reacting from that place.

Your actions, behaviors, and experiences are often driven
by past traumas and the unconscious parts of yourself.

When you begin to understand your unconscious traumas, you start to understand yourself better. We cannot blame everything that happened to us on our parents or the people who raised us, because they too were products of their own upbringing. They passed on to us what they knew and what they believed was true or right.

They were likely just as confused as you were about their own behavior toward you. Because they had little knowledge or understanding of their own internal traumas and unconscious patterns, they continued to do what they believed was right for them.

I don't believe that any parents—unless they are mentally ill or unstable—ever intentionally mean to hurt their own children.

We are all victims of victims. Our parents were themselves shaped by hurtful environments that made them the way they are. They may have been hurting all along or suffering from unresolved traumas from their own past. I recognized this in my own parents.

Their way of parenting reflected how they had been parented by their own parents. In turn, I inherited these patterns and, without realizing it, recreated the same life dynamics in my own life.

When I became aware of my depression, I realized that, unconsciously, I had spent much of my life in a state of severe depression. The physical effects of this were reflected in my unconscious choices, repetitive mistakes, and destructive behaviors and relationships.

It is impossible to escape the state of darkness when you are carrying unresolved, painful traumas. Unhealed internal wounds or unconscious traumas will always manifest in your current life—often in painful ways and triggered unexpectedly. I know this from my many profound experiences on my healing journey.

Most people experiencing real depression remain stuck in that state because they are unaware of its root causes. The first step is to become conscious and aware of what is happening inside you—by acknowledging what you notice within yourself or by reflecting on past life events.

Where have you been over the last five, ten, fifteen, or twenty years? What repetitive patterns or destructive behaviors have you engaged in without recognizing them—until you found yourself in the midst of chaos or catastrophe?

If you take the time to sit quietly and ask yourself honestly, what are the things that are keeping me depressed? — you may discover that your depression is sending you many messages, if only you are willing to sit with it and listen.

I remember feeling unbearably heavy, glued to anything I could sit or lie on, as if something was trying to keep me still. You are in that state because something is holding you, urging you to pay close attention to what it is trying to tell you.

- What is it?

- How do you truly feel about yourself and your life right now?

- What are you holding onto inside that you cannot let go of?

- Where are your anger and resentment coming from?

- Who is the person you wish you had never met?

- Is your job draining you?

- What is going on with your children, your parents, or your siblings?

- Have you lost connection with the things you used to enjoy or love doing?

- Do you still feel the heavy-hearted from a divorce, separation, or a break-up that happened years ago?

- Are you still holding onto the hate and resentment toward someone who hurt you years ago?

- Have you lost your self-respect and self-worth because you feel unworthy or invisible to others?

- Have you lost the strength to fight, to stand up, or to speak up for yourself?

What is your depression telling you right now? Sit with it and be willing to listen, because that is where you will find your answers.

IS MEDICATION REALLY WHAT YOU NEED?

If you have been taking medications, now is the time to sit down and be completely honest about how they are affecting you. Have you become numb, lost your sense of reality, or do you feel that no matter what you do, the pain and struggle persist every day?

Or is the medication something you genuinely believe is helping you cope with daily life challenges—or is it crippling you, making you feel worse rather than better?

Only you can decide if medication is truly the path you want to take, knowing that medications **Do Not** cure this natural human condition called depression.

Depression existed long before antidepressant medications were created. People in those times learned to live with it and still function fully, because medications were not an option or were not as readily available as they are today.

Today, many people are misdiagnosed with various "disorders" and treated with the wrong medications. I know many who have been through this journey and can attest that, for them, the medications actually worsened their condition.

Taking any addictive substance—including these powerful prescribed medications—can eventually lead to dependence. Not only do they fail to heal your depression, but you also face the additional struggle of overcoming addiction to the medications themselves.

Only you can truly know, based on how you feel, whether medication is something you really need because you cannot cope with what you are going through without it. I personally know a few people who chose to medicate themselves because they didn't want to face the reality or the root cause of their depression.

> Often, we already know what is causing our pain, but we avoid confronting the reality of uncomfortable or painful situations.

At the depth of my depression, I felt helpless, powerless, and overwhelmed, trying to make sense of what was happening to me. One day, I even considered seeing a doctor to be prescribed something, because I felt I had reached the limit of my capacity to tolerate the agonizing pain of depression.

By that time, I had already educated myself enough about medications, so for several reasons, the thought of seeing a doctor terrified me. Each time I felt like giving up, I ended up finding other ways to comfort myself instead.

> Recognizing my inner power—the ability to stop myself even in my weakest moments—was profoundly meaningful. It often helped me discover a sense of inner strength, which then led me to choose healthier ways to comfort myself.

Many people take medications for various reasons, and often for the wrong ones. You may be in deep despair and simply want to escape to avoid emotional discomfort, but deep down, you know when something is doing more harm than good.

Before choosing the path of medication, sit down and ask yourself honestly: Do you really need medication, and why do you believe you need it? Truth and radical self-honesty are what set us free.

If you decide to take the path of medicating the symptoms of depression, understand that medication can only help to a certain extent. The longer you rely on it, the more difficult it can become to step away from it. Medication **does not** heal depression.

It may numb your symptoms and stabilize you temporarily, but in the long run, it can also limit your growth and emotional awareness. Do not experiment on yourself by trying different medications just to find instant relief.

You need to give yourself the chance to truly understand what is going on inside you and why you are in despair—desperately seeking instant relief to feel better.

The real cure for depression lies in learning about your condition, understanding it, and healing its roots.

Now is the time to face your own life's battle, win it for yourself, and give yourself the love and care you deserve—something we often forget while trying to love everyone around us but neglecting ourselves.

You carry your own body, feel your own emotions, and think your own thoughts. Every second, you have the power to choose which way to go. Change begins the moment you decide to help yourself and truly be there for yourself.

Begin with small steps every day, no matter how minor they may seem. Start by doing things that make you feel better each day, no matter what you choose to do. It could be something as simple as taking a long bath if you haven't done so in days.

Reconnect with the good feelings you used to have. You might start writing down how you feel each day if you have no one to talk to regularly or allow yourself to cry whenever you feel heavy inside. Crying helps release the tension we hold in our bodies.

We often feel lighter after letting go of heavy emotions. Physical movement can also shift our emotional state. Even something as simple as walking around your home or changing your usual environment—where you often feel triggered—can help. Try sitting in a different part of your home each day to create small shifts in perspective.

As you become more conscious and aware of what is happening inside you, you can build momentum by making a daily effort to do new things that help you feel better. Anything counts. Try going outside, even if it's just to sit somewhere new and unfamiliar.

When we are in a state of depression, we often become disconnected from reality because we are so focused on dwelling on the symptoms that keep us feeling low. One of the most effective ways to break this cycle is through physical movement—by constantly changing our physical state.

That is why exercise is often recommended as a natural and immediate way to feel better. Immobility and physical exhaustion are common symptoms of depression, and movement helps counteract them.

If you don't learn to rely on yourself, you may continue to feel helpless, hopeless, and powerless. Now is the time to trust yourself and believe in your ability to rise above this very challenging condition called depression.

CHAPTER 12

FROM PAIN AND SUFFERING TO LOVE AND FORGIVENESS

I discovered my own healing in the deepest, darkest trenches of my depression by staying fully awake and experiencing every detail of that journey.

Healing any type of wound or trauma—both internal and external—is an embodied process. It happens in the details, in the fleeting glimpses of experience. Healing is found in how conscious and present you are.

It comes from feeling and embodying profound experiences that can only be sensed, felt, and discovered in solitude or in moments of quiet, undistracted attention—where you can connect with experiences that only you can recognize.

Hearing others share their journeys through depression also helped me understand my own pain and played a significant role in my healing. By placing myself in their position to understand them better, I found that healing became effortless.

By understanding where your pain comes from, you help others as much as you help yourself. You demonstrate this strength and dignity by meeting people where they are. When you are healed, you gain the capacity to hold and process pain—not only your own, but also the pain of others—through understanding.

This is something I never knew I was capable of or even imagined was possible. Throughout the healing journey, you begin to experience love and forgiveness naturally and simultaneously, without forcing it.

When you become internally whole and healthy, you start to connect with people on a much deeper level. Once you emerge from the darkness of pain and suffering, you become more sensitive to it in others—and more compassionate in how you respond.

When you are healed, you will easily recognize the separation between light and darkness—or between positive and negative energy around you—because you have experienced and been through it all. Everything in our world exists to help us understand the difference.

Healing is not a destination; it is a lifelong journey and a lifestyle that we must adapt to and master. No matter how healthy or healed we believe we are, life will continue with its ups and downs.

We are all part of this dynamic for as long as we are alive. Both good and bad experiences are always present for our conscious choosing. By recognizing this truth, you hold the power to decide which emotions to embrace and which to release or let go.

You cannot experience both at the same time. So, stay aware—so you can choose wisely—and do so intentionally.

Healing ourselves is the only true way out of depression. When you choose the path of self-healing, you will encounter parts of yourself that you never knew existed—or that you have forgotten or neglected.

You will cultivate strengths and capacities within yourself that you never realized you had. You will reconnect with the part of yourself that has always been waiting for you—your True Self, your unique identity, or your personal blueprint.

You will recognize it when you arrive. It feels true, natural, loving, and freeing. You will experience your very own human nature—and how effortless, beautiful, and meaningful life can be—once you come to know every part of yourself.

The path to discovering who you truly are and understanding your own nature exists only through healing. We will never fully know ourselves if we are trapped in suffering, because pain blocks the way.

Healing trauma means transforming all your pain and suffering into true inner happiness and inner strength. Healing yourself and coming to terms with everything that has happened to you is the only way to experience the brighter side of life. It is impossible to be truly happy and fulfilled if pain stands in the way.

As you heal, you clear your path and sharpen your vision, allowing you to see things clearly. Your perception of life changes—and being internally healthy helps you make better choices. You become more conscious and aware, able to distinguish right from wrong with greater clarity.

You begin to see everything as it truly is, no longer filtered through the pain, delusions, or broken beliefs created by trauma.

The moment you take that first step toward healing, you begin to feel and experience a sense of hope, freedom, or liberation. When you become internally whole and healthy, you will understand that happiness and suffering are ultimately choices.

However, you cannot recognize this or apply it while living in a state of pain and suffering. Once you are internally healthy, you will better understand the pain and joy of others.

Your jealousy will fade, and envy will transform into genuine appreciation and applause for others' achievements—because you now understand what it takes to achieve something.

Becoming healthy is a remarkable personal achievement, one that many may never reach, because it requires a tremendous amount of internal courage to heal the wounds within.

The moment you understand your own pain, you begin to understand others, because we all share the same longing to feel better. You become more compassionate and empathetic toward others simply because you now understand.

There are stages of healing. Some days will feel better than others, while on other days the process can feel excruciating. Old wounds or traumas may be triggered by people or events in the present that resemble past experiences.

When painful memories are triggered, you may experience the same pain all over again. Being open to feeling these emotional discomforts and staying engaged and aware of what is happening inside you—primarily how you feel moment by moment—is the key to continuous healing.

When you are aware, you can respond **consciously** rather than acting unconsciously or aimlessly. Staying aware, exploring your experiences, and applying what you learn will give you a sense of hope and the strength to keep going.

The healing experience can feel more painful precisely because you are now fully aware of your pain. This is a natural part of the healing process that you must allow to happen and let pass through you—rather than avoiding, running from, or resisting it.

Each time you work through an emotional pain or discomfort, you emerge healthier. This is why many people in recovery relapse and return to familiar pain: healing, especially in the early stages, can be overwhelming and excruciating.

The secret of healing is learning to become comfortable with the discomfort of pain.

You will know and sense within yourself when you are truly getting healthier. You will feel lighter and stronger, begin to feel better, and notice yourself becoming calmer, more loving, and more caring.

Healing could mean:

- Letting go of all your past experiences that continue to hurt you and keep you in a state of suffering. You are now ready to create a better future while enjoying the process.

- Taking full responsibility for your own life, happiness, and well-being. You are now ready to repair relationships that have been broken, whether due to conscious or unconscious choices or mistakes.

- Walking away from the wrong people, meaningless relationships, and environments that continue to hurt you and no longer serve you.

- Letting go of the need to control everything you cannot control. You are now ready to experience the other side of life—the side that is free from pain and suffering.

- Changing the direction of every area of your life, because you are ready to be happy, to thrive, and to live the best life possible—while becoming the best version of yourself.

- Never allowing anything or anyone to hurt you again. You are now ready to like and love yourself, care for yourself, and fulfill your own needs—before caring for and fulfilling the needs of others.

Healing could also mean becoming conscious and aware of what is happening both inside and outside of you. Healing yourself is the path to a better and brighter tomorrow, because as you heal, you clear the dark path before you.

You develop the ability to make better choices and decisions because you are now aware of your thoughts, actions, and intentions—resulting in fewer aimless actions and unconscious mistakes.

When you become whole and internally healthy, you connect with people more easily and on a deeper level than before. By understanding every part of yourself, you gain the capacity to understand others more deeply. You become truly connected to life and the people around you.

As you become more conscious, you begin to experience life on a much higher plane. You start to see how vast life truly is—bigger than you could have imagined. New possibilities will open up for you to step into. So, keep going.

FORGIVENESS AUTOMATICALLY HAPPENS AS YOU HEAL YOURSELF

As a young girl growing up, constantly hurt and traumatized, I was very confused and couldn't understand why my father seemed to take pleasure in torturing me.

Yet even as a little girl, I had a deep sense of knowing—an inner awareness of what was true about the person or the situation—despite everything that was happening and everything people were doing to me and around me.

As I was healing myself and revisiting every agonizing moment of my past—remembering vividly the different faces, characters, personalities, and behaviors of the people who hurt me—I wanted to convince myself that they were heartless and inhumane.

Yet I could not deny that I had also sensed moments of something different in them. There were times when I saw them in their most vulnerable state, treating me in kind, gentle, and most sincere ways.

Even the people who raped and sexually abused me—truth is truth. No matter how much we try to twist it or deny it, the reality remains.

Now, having experienced both internal health and the lack thereof, I understand that both I and my abusers were painfully and desperately trying to survive.

Our pain and suffering—our sense of longing, emptiness, and desperation—met in those moments. Their pain and desperation were the driving forces behind their behavior toward me, and my silent compliance came from fear and the desire not to get hurt.

As I became more conscious and aware of my past traumas, the memories of people from my dark past suddenly came alive, haunting me all at once. My first reaction was intense anger toward them.

But after years of healing, studying, and understanding my own pain and suffering, all of that slowly fell away. Forgiveness—or even the need for an apology—became unnecessary and irrelevant.

My broad understanding of human brutality is that it stems from pain and suffering. By knowing my own pain and understanding the roots of my suffering, I now know—without a doubt—that all humans are inherently good.

They have simply been hurt. As traumatizing and agonizing as my childhood was, I came to understand that my father, my mother, and every person who hurt me—whether intentionally or unintentionally—were just as much in pain and suffering as I was.

No happy, whole, mentally sane, and rational person would purposely hurt another. All harmful behaviors are driven by pain, suffering, or desperation.

As a very confused young girl, wondering why my father—who was supposed to love, protect, and care for me—was hurting me, I never once doubted, and still don't, that both my parents loved me and deeply cared about me.

I also never doubted that the people who hurt me intentionally—including the men who abducted, raped, and sexually abused me—acted out of their own pain or desperation to survive.

I saw the sorrow and suffering in each of them during moments when they showed weakness, kindness, gentleness, or vulnerability. In those moments, I saw the good in them. But I also know and acknowledge that recognizing vulnerability behind anyone's callous actions doesn't make them right.

The excruciating part of the healing process is confronting every truth that surfaces—truths you cannot deny. It is when you realize that in everything that happened to you, you were a part—both consciously and unconsciously, but mostly unconsciously—through the ways you reacted and responded. We often react to life unconsciously.

When I woke up to the reality of my life, I realized that I had lost my emotional connection with the people I love and value most—but they had never truly left my life.

I was emotionally and psychologically detached from them the entire time. I was expressing my love from a place of being wounded, hurt, broken, lost, and empty. I was numb and blinded by my own pain and suffering.

> I was doing everything for the wrong reasons, searching desperately for any possible way to feel better.

The agonizing pain of depression and the healing journey forced me to recognize and physically experience decades of anguish, internal rage, and suppressed hatred that came from feeling deeply hurt, betrayed, and victimized—until I became mentally and emotionally drained and physically weak and fragile.

It felt like I was approaching my lowest point of tolerance. Then, a sudden shift happened inside me, as if someone had gently poked me with a needle. I suddenly felt like I wanted to fly and be free. This was the moment I realized I had reached the end of my suffering.

The first two words that came out of my mouth were "Thank You," followed by uncontrollable sobbing—and then a sense of immediate freedom and relief.

I felt light and free. Through this profoundly transformative experience, I came to understand and feel the sense of "flying" without wings.

Forgiveness becomes effortless, and pain and suffering
naturally fall away when you understand where all your
pain is coming from—not only your own, but also the
pain of those who hurt you.

Even during the first thirteen years of my life, when I was tortured by my own father like a powerless and helpless captive child, I came to understand that it all happened for me.

The deeply ingrained pain and suffering from my childhood humbled me and brought me to my knees when I finally became fully awake and aware of my past.

I realized how deeply wounded I was—yet I still managed to stand up and continue fighting. Each time I felt like giving up, something new and miraculous happened that kept me moving forward.

I took full responsibility for my life because I was physically present when everything happened, whether I had consciously chosen to be there or not.

The wounded and unconscious part of me was watching everything that was happening, while I was physically present and unknowingly participating in it all.

When I recognized that I was behaving and reacting from my unconscious trauma, I let go of my external battles and turned inward—toward the place where all the roots existed.

Then everything began to cooperate with me. I discovered my infinite inner resources in the depths of my depression. I surrendered to the process as I continued my healing journey.

One day, I realized that I had resolved what was unresolved, found answers to my unanswered questions, and cleared my confusion. I began to sense that everything was aligning to support me, as if life itself were bending to help me move forward—without force or struggle.

I began to feel better as I grew healthier, and I started to sense my pain transforming into wisdom, compassion, and understanding. I now know that we are all just victims of victims—the products of our own upbringing, which we did not consciously choose.

My father suffered for as long as he could endure his illness, brought on by his severe alcohol addiction. Witnessing his vulnerability as he battled his own struggles, I asked myself: Who am I to even be angry at him? His addiction had taken over his ability and will to help himself.

Even when he was physically able, he didn't have the will to change. Only when I became conscious and aware of my past did I realize that I had watched my father destroy himself until the day he passed away. The impact of that experience on my own life was far deeper than I had ever understood.

Understanding the root cause of my own suffering helped me understand why hurt people hurt others. A person cannot truly love if pain is all they carry in their heart. Hurting others becomes a way to relieve their own pain and suffering. I resonated with their pain because I had been one of them.

I was unconsciously seeking to feel better in any way I could. As part of my healing, revisiting my past allowed me to recognize that I had been responding and reacting to life unconsciously—until the day I had a panic attack and woke up to the reality of my life. I became fully, completely awake.

Most people go through life unconscious or half-asleep. When you begin to heal yourself, you start to sense the true reality of this existence.

It becomes almost impossible to blame or judge anyone, knowing that they often don't understand what they are doing—and realizing that this could easily be **You**.

One major part of my healing was understanding why people hurt others. The more I understood it; the more effortless forgiveness became. When you forgive from a place of understanding, resentment naturally vanishes.

You realize that most people are not fully aware of their behaviors. It may seem like they are, but the truth is that most act from a place of pain and desperation, trying to fill the voids within themselves to survive—and I was once one of those people.

When you forgive from a place of understanding, explanations or apologies may be nice, but they become irrelevant or unnecessary because you already know the answers.

Understanding and letting go does not mean you must continue associating with anyone who is hurtful or destructive, nor does it mean you need to forget what happened. It simply means that you no longer allow the past to affect you or continue to hurt you.

Knowing what I know now about unconscious traumas, no matter how we feel about those who have wronged or hurt us, their behavior comes from their own pain and suffering.

Hurting others becomes their way of coping because pain is all they know. They comfort themselves in the only ways they understand. We all act similarly when we are in pain. Understanding and accepting this truth is, in itself, an act of forgiving them—without even having to confront them.

The only person we need to constantly forgive is ourselves—for allowing those people and situations to continue affecting us, even when it all seemingly makes no sense.

Every hurtful or destructive behavior is driven by pain, suffering, or desperation as part of a person's survival. This could even be you at this very moment.

Radical and unconditional self-forgiveness—for how we have treated ourselves all these years—is what we all need to give ourselves. It has been us who have treated ourselves unfairly by holding on to pain and allowing ourselves to suffer for so long.

Whether we are aware of it or not, no matter how much we blame others or our circumstances, what has happened cannot be changed.

We cannot wait for someone to rescue us, for another person to change, to apologize, or to save us. That day may never come. Meanwhile, we continue to miss the opportunities that are right in front of us—the opportunities to heal, improve our own lives, and create healthy relationships.

Most people get stuck living in the past, hoping for something to get better, waiting for someone to change, or wishing for things to be different—and I was one of them.

Don't be one of those people who spend their lives waiting for miracles to save them. We create our own miracles by taking full responsibility for everything that has happened and everything that is happening in our lives.

CHAPTER 13

TRUTH, MIRACLES, AND FREEDOM

When you are healed and learn to live in your own truth and follow your inner convictions, you feel free and liberated. You free yourself from everything that has kept you stuck or imprisoned.

Freedom can mean:

- **Releasing the past**—choosing to let go of anything that holds you back from moving forward in life.

- **Allowing others their path**—letting people live their lives and walk their chosen paths without judgment or condemnation.

- **Not being controlled by others**—choosing not to be affected by what people think, say, or do. You are no longer controlled by anything or anyone that causes you pain or prevents you from enjoying life.

- **Letting go of control**—releasing the need to manage everything and everyone, allowing them to be as they are, regardless of their actions or relationship to you. Healing is not about changing others—it is about becoming better and healthier ourselves.

- **Surrendering the battle**—giving up the fight against situations or people you cannot control.

- **Freeing yourself from toxicity**—choosing to step away from people or circumstances that leave you feeling paralyzed, helpless, or hopeless.

Living in your truths can mean:

- Accepting everything that has happened to you and everything that is happening in your life—regardless of the actions or involvement of others.

- Honoring reality and living according to what feels true to you, even if your truths do not align with the narratives of those around you.

- Releasing the need to prove yourself—stopping the urge to care, explain, or justify anything to anyone. You are ready to live in what you know is true, whether or not others believe you.

- Making peace with the past—coming to terms with your mistakes and accepting what cannot be changed. You are now ready to forgive yourself and let go of guilt, shame, or regrets caused by conscious or unconscious choices.

- Choosing inner peace—remaining at peace with yourself and everything that has happened, even when those truths are difficult to accept.

The word "**miracle**" used to mean nothing more to me than "wishful thinking"—hoping for something unimaginable to happen without truly believing it. Healing, unlike suffering, carries a similar subtle sense of the miraculous—small realizations that something good has just occurred.

These moments often appeared when I gave myself mental space and allowed myself to ask questions while fully feeling the pain of my past. I remember noticing my surroundings growing brighter, seeing myself move with more ease, feeling lighter each day, and slowly coming alive again.

I became so aware that even the smallest things began to amuse me—things I had never noticed or cared about before.

I remember sitting on a bench with my five-year-old daughter while waiting for the store to open. A line of tiny ants was crossing the bench—and for the first time in my life, I was mesmerized, watching them struggle for microscopic pieces of breadcrumbs.

I was so amused and found meaning in their efforts. I saw life in those tiny creatures.

When you are free from pain and suffering, you begin to find meaning in every experience—from the smallest to the largest.

When you become awake and receptive to all of life's moments, your senses are heightened, and even the tiniest things can make you giggle.

The miraculous moments of amusement and experience often left me lost in spaces I had never known before. The reality of these experiences is so vivid and deeply felt that words alone cannot fully capture them.

I grew up near the ocean, surrounded by beaches, beautiful hills and mountains, streams, rivers, and waterfalls. They were my playgrounds, yet I had forgotten these joyful childhood memories after leaving home at thirteen.

As I began to feel internally healthy, for the first time since leaving home, I longed to reconnect with those places—especially the beaches. I wanted to walk barefoot on the sand, to remember the happiest part of my childhood, a time when I was free and unafraid.

A time when I had so much fun and feared nothing—before returning to a home filled with torture, terror, and the dark side of life.

The healthier I became, the more miracles—or unexplainable events—began appearing in my everyday life. I became deeply receptive to everything, open to whatever life offered me to experience. Even unwanted or unpleasant situations were met with acceptance.

I found myself searching for meaning, seeking the lessons these experiences had to teach me. My anger subsided, and my love, compassion, and empathy toward others grew so unconditional that no matter how people behaved, all I felt was understanding.

I realized that behind every behavior lies a suppressed emotion someone is holding inside and longing to express. I learned to let them express themselves as they choose, knowing that I don't need to be part of anyone else's painful emotional experiences.

I discovered the secret to fully experiencing what it means to be truly human. I learned to process the entire gamut of emotions—whether happiness, joy, anger, disappointment, or frustration—whatever arises. I welcome each emotion, feel it fully, and stay with it until it passes through my entire body.

Then I seek the meaning behind every experience and the reasons it has been presented to me. Every emotional experience carries its own message or purpose.

> I learned never to hold on to any experience longer than it wants to stay, because holding on has been one of the causes of my greatest suffering—clinging to emotions that no longer belong in my body.

I learned to let go of every person when they need to go, including my own children. I learned to detach from every occasion or event when its moment has ended.

> True freedom arises when you no longer cater to, participate in, allow, or accept anything that disturbs your spirit.

When you become internally healthy, you come to deeply appreciate and value living in peace—free from pain and suffering.

When you learn to live in your own convictions, you learn to stand up for what you believe in. You honor what feels true to you while respectfully honoring others for doing the same.

There is nothing to explain and nothing to prove to anyone, because your truths are the only things that truly matter.

Miracles happen when you start taking action, even without signs or assurances that things will change or get better. You act simply because where you are no longer serves you.

You act with trust and faith—trusting the uncertainty and letting go of worry about the outcome. Close your eyes and just trust.

Miracles—or the unexpected—happen when you give them space to enter your life—when you let go of everything and allow life to unfold.

Most of our pain and suffering comes from dwelling on what hurts us, making living in pain a habit or a way of life. Healing begins the moment you accept the reality of what has happened and what is happening in your life—and understand why it all had to happen.

Freedom is the reward for everything you consciously and wholeheartedly do with pure intentions. Miracles will appear right before your eyes the moment you turn your focus away from what is hurting you.

Live life with an open heart and mind and allow life to show you what true freedom and miracles feel like.

When you become whole, healthy, and complete, you are literally living on a higher plane of life. This makes you highly sensitive to anything that brings you joy or lifts your spirits. This is what it means to be "high on life."

You become deeply receptive to everything that feels good. As you heal yourself, good things begin to happen to those around you because of the positive energy you create. When you are internally aware and healthy, every word you speak and every thought you have toward anyone is first felt within yourself.

You become mindful of everything you do because you experience it internally before others sense it. And when you are fully aware of what is happening both inside and outside of you, you gain the ability to protect yourself.

Miracles are the moments or glimpses of unexplainable experiences, both within and around you, that occur when you are free of pain and open to receive them.

Freedom and liberation are the feelings of being truly free—when you let go of everything that feels painful and heavy.

So, what happens when you finally take the path to heal all your unresolved emotional and psychological traumas—or internal wounds—through understanding?

- You find justice for all the injustices people inflicted on you and for all the events in your life—without punishing anyone, especially yourself. Justice comes naturally when you understand how things happened through your moral awareness. Because when you truly know, you just know.

- Everything in your life begins to shift, and you wake up each day feeling relieved and free, because you are no longer bound by unnecessary pain and suffering.

- You see the world differently, as your perceptions of reality become clearer. You observe what is happening around you as it truly is, no longer filtered through pain, false beliefs, illusions, or delusions caused by past traumas.

- You get to know who you truly are. By understanding every part of yourself, you also come to understand humanity as a whole and how we are all connected.

- Relationships that were broken when you were broken begin to repair themselves naturally.

- You attract new people who resonate with you as you develop your new identity and evolve into the person you choose to become.

- People from your past who no longer align with your energy gradually fall away as you get healthier.

- Those who have wronged you may begin to recognize their own behavior and reflect on themselves as they witness the changes in you.

- You embrace and appreciate all kinds of experiences as essential parts of life journey.

- You develop a deeper sense of responsibility, accountability, and independence.

- You become more compassionate and understanding toward others, because now that you know better, you truly understand.

CHAPTER 14

I BROKE THE CHAINS AND MADE IT THROUGH

Healing means reconciling with ourselves—and with all our unresolved past experiences and everything beyond our control—so that we can move forward in life. It is impossible to create a better, happier life from a place of pain and suffering.

Unresolved trauma—both conscious and unconscious—will inevitably show up in everything we do. These damaging energies remain in our system until we confront them, come to terms with them, and make peace with them.

I have witnessed this in my own life when I tried to "forget" everything and simply move on. The past continued to haunt me and influenced everything I did because my behavior was still driven by pain and trauma.

This is something none of us can deny, whether we are aware of it or not: our behaviors are always shaped by what we carry inside, by how we feel internally, and by how we feel about ourselves.

If pain is what you carry, you will always operate, react, and respond from that place—until you resolve it and reconcile with it.

Healing all forms of internal, emotional, and psychological trauma is a lifestyle that must be practiced every day. It is, therefore, a lifelong journey. Healing and recovery are entirely internal processes—work that only you can do.

Years of medication, medical treatments, psychological therapy or counseling, and even natural or spiritual healing can help only to a certain extent. They can support us, but they can only take us so far in our healing and recovery.

In the end, we are always left with our own truth when none of these external guides or supports are present. Truth speaks the loudest when we are alone—when we are the only ones listening and sensing what is happening within us.

Throughout my healing journey, it often felt as though I was being guided by nature through profound experiences and spontaneous flashes of memories. I became so attuned to my inner state that I could sense every subtle shift and every deep transformation within me.

Each change and internal shift kept me intensely curious about what was happening inside. That curiosity led me to pieces of the puzzle, eventually guiding me along the path of healing and recovery—and ultimately to a complete transformation of myself and my entire life.

I suffered from all types of abuse for most of the thirty-nine years of my life—not just minor abuses, but crippling, compounded forms of abuse. When I realized how deeply crippled I was internally, I didn't know where to begin.

Looking back now at how my healing began, I see that powerful panic attack as my "wake-up call." It shook me so profoundly and intensely that I could not ignore it. That intense experience of awakening compelled me to search for its meaning.

Having carried that deep sense of knowing since I was a little girl, I had learned how to constantly save myself and survive the very hostile environment I grew up in—living under constant threat, poverty, violence, and hostility every hour of every day.

The moment I felt the courage to step out of our house at thirteen, I left—with nothing but that deep sense of knowing that I needed to be somewhere else. Leaving home was just the end of one chapter and the beginning of many more agonizing life tests that I had to endure to reach where I am today.

So, when you find yourself feeling like there is no way out of a situation, always remember that you are not alone. Most people live in survival mode for all kinds of reasons. So don't continue to feel victimized or helpless.

Your life is your own path to navigate, your own battles to win, and yours to experience and enjoy however you choose. I never thought I could ever get myself out of that state of depression.

But understanding this truth after years of healing and recovery—that I hold the power to create the life and environment I want to live in—led me to the right place in life.

My personal journey of healing and recovery brought me to a place I still can't fully comprehend to this day. The freedom and liberation that come from living a life free of pain and suffering are things I never even knew existed—because pain and suffering had been all I had ever known.

I lived in a state of severe depression for thirty-nine years, caused by my past traumas. I didn't know any other way to live or experience life beyond what I absorbed and learned at home and the life my parents modeled for us.

I had absolutely no knowledge of emotional wounds or psychological trauma—let alone how to heal myself—until that powerful panic attack activated it all. The profound realization that only I could get myself out of my suffering was what finally pushed me to do the work.

Knowing that no one—and absolutely no one—was coming to save me from my pain and life struggles is what made me get up, start moving, and keep going, no matter how agonizing the healing journey was.

> My senses, my intuition, my gut instinct, and my inner knowing were all I had to guide me—telling me where to go and what to do next.

It can be incredibly difficult to accept our painful pasts and face our own flaws, mistakes, and failings—especially when it feels like others are the ones who have wronged us.

So, we stay feeling victimized by others or by circumstances. I spent years blaming everything and everyone for what happened to me. It took me years to realize and accept that I had participated in it all—whether I was aware of it or not. I forgave myself and came to terms with everything.

Now, after almost a decade of deliberate healing practice—embodying and consciously healing every part of my wounded being—I can finally say, Hallelujah.

The healing process was the most excruciating journey of my life. But it was the path I needed to walk in order to reach the other side of that very dark life. And with the grace of ever-loving and infinitely forgiving Life, I am now living free of unnecessary pain and suffering—feeling whole, healthy, and complete. **I BROKE THE CHAIN.**

I emerged from decades of trauma and shattered the cycles of generational pain. I healed the wounds I had absorbed, endured, and carried for thirty-nine years. **I MADE IT THROUGH.**

FROM THAT LOST, FRIGHTENED, AND VULNERABLE YOUNG GIRL AND RAPED VICTIM TO MY OWN SAVIOR AND HERO.

The child who lived in terror, brutality, hostility, and the most dysfunctional home environment for thirteen years—and the fear I felt every time my second ex-husband threatened me to leave the house—activated memories of growing up horrified, with nowhere to go.

Now, I have created a home for myself and my loved ones where we can comfortably and peacefully go to sleep at night, knowing that we are safe and secure—a home I never had. Safe, happy, peaceful, and free from terror, hostility, and destruction.

As I healed myself from my childhood and rape traumas, a former male client, whom I had not seen or heard from in years, crossed my path again. This time, I got to know him well. I knew this person previously; he was battling depression and multiple addictions.

After spending some time with him, I recognized very familiar traits—his character, personality, and behavior were similar to the men who sexually abused me. As part of my healing process and revisiting past events, I took advantage of this opportunity and befriended him to closely observe his behavior.

After some time, he began to behave very inappropriately, which triggered many memories of narcissistic behavior and reminded me of the men who raped and sexually abused me, because of their strikingly similar behaviors and personalities.

By observing this person's behavior and how unconscious he was, I found the answers I needed to close the missing gaps of my unresolved sexual abuse trauma. With him, I recognized how much I had grown. I walked away peacefully.

One night, another familiar incident occurred—while I was on a dinner date with a very kind and much older gentleman, I realized that I was there to confront the last traces of my past trauma: my unmet need for a father and the reason I had been raped by older men.

Sitting at the dinner table in a fine dining restaurant, facing this gentleman, I suddenly recognized that the missing piece of me—the need for a father—was no longer there. I was on the date for the wrong reason. So, I politely said goodbye, because all I wanted was to go home.

As I was driving home, realizing what had just happened, I felt a heavy weight lift from my body. I recognized that my trauma—the longing for love from a father—had finally left me. I realized that I had been parenting myself so well as I healed my childhood wounds.

I had been so consumed by my healing journey, every step of the way, that I hadn't noticed how much I was progressing.

When you are healed and internally healthy, there is nothing outside of yourself that can complete or fulfill you. Feeling whole and complete becomes your state of being. And when you feel whole and complete, there is nothing to fill—because there is no space or gap left empty. **I MADE IT.**

FROM THE NEGLECTED, LOST, AND LONELY CHILD WHO NEEDED A MOTHER TO BECOMING MY OWN MOTHER.

Healing internal wounds or traumas feels like peeling layers of an onion. You keep going, and you keep crying, until you reach the core—and there is nothing left to peel. That is when you know you have made it through.

The deepest part of my healing was meeting the child within me who had been neglected, lost, abandoned, lonely, and carrying decades of unconscious longings for deep connection—waiting to be parented, cared for, and comforted.

This was the most excruciating part of my healing because it was the part of my life I did not want to remember or revisit. Yet this part is the very core of our healing, because this is where our deepest wounds lie and where the true nature of who we are resides: **the child within us.**

I grew up in a very remote area, where neighbors were a few miles apart, but I had lots of people around me—my cousins and other family members. My mother had eleven siblings, and my father had three brothers, and we all lived within the same vicinity.

When our parents were away, we would play far from our homes until sunset. Healing my childhood wounds brought back that best part of my early life—the part of me that had been lost, neglected, and overshadowed by painful and traumatic experiences.

Now I am back in that childlike state: carefree, happy, playful, and lighthearted, where anything can make me giggle—or even cry. But now, I carry all the life wisdom I have gained, which I will forever live by.

I am now the parent to that child within me. I am there to comfort her when she needs it and to guide her when she needs discipline. I found my mother—the parent I had been searching for all my life. I found myself. The best mother I could possibly be for myself. **I MADE IT THROUGH.**

FROM BEING REACTIVE AND HYPER-VIGILANT TO BEING CALM, RESPONSIVE, AND REGULATED.

I lived the first thirty-nine years of my life in the darkness of pain, suffering, sadness, and fear—constantly frightened and hyper-vigilant. It was as if someone were always after me, as if something terrible was always about to happen, and my inner rage was like a "ticking time bomb," ready to explode at any moment.

As I healed my psychological and emotional traumas, understanding where they came from and what triggered my uncontrollable reactions, everything slowly began to fall away as I became healthier.

My deep understanding of my past traumas and how they connect to my present life has made the process of healing feel almost effortless.

Now, when I get triggered by something, it doesn't mean I don't react. I still feel anxious, nervous, and afraid. And yes, I still get angry or frustrated—but now I am aware and understand where my reactions are coming from. They are either rooted in my unconscious traumas or simply arise from my human nature, trying to protect me.

It's that part of ourselves that automatically activates our fight, flight, or freeze response whenever we encounter something new or unfamiliar—triggering feelings of fear, discomfort, anxiety, or nervousness.

Growing up, all I knew was to suppress my emotions as a way to cope. I mastered the ability to keep myself quiet whenever my father physically hurt me—no matter how much pain I felt. I believe this skill is what ultimately saved me and kept me alive from my rapists and other abusers.

I quietly felt and sensed everything that was happening to me, even when I desperately wanted to scream, because I feared they would hurt me even more. Now, I can easily and comfortably regulate my emotions as they arise and no longer react uncontrollably.

I can express my anger and frustrations assertively, without being consumed by them. Through healing every wounded part of myself, I discovered my true nature and reclaimed every missing piece of myself that had been stripped away by traumatic life events.

I am now on the other side of that darkness caused by decades of anguish, pain, grief, and sorrow. How do I know that? I now live my life in faith, trusting the darkness of the unknown. Because I know that if I ever get lost in the dark again, I will always find my way out—because I have been there many times.

I now enjoy my life fully in the reality of every present moment—not in the absence of anything. Every day, I wake up before dawn, sipping my favorite cup of amaretto-flavored coffee while looking out through my bay window at the beautiful colors of the sky as the sun slowly rises.

I remember the moments when I felt safest and happiest, sitting beside my grandfather in front of our early morning campfire—when I visited him between the ages of six and nine.

Always excited and ready for another day of adventure, never worrying about how my day would end, because I knew that tomorrow would bring yet another day of adventure.

This is how my daily life has become. Every day is a new day to begin again, regardless of what happened in the past or yesterday. Every day is a new beginning. **I MADE IT.**

FROM THAT SIX-YEAR-OLD GIRL WHO WAS TERRIFIED OF ANIMALS TO LOVING EVERY LIVING THING.

I was bitten by a big dog when I was six years old, and I carried that terrifying trauma with me until I encountered a very similar dog along my healing journey.

I had been terrified of all types of animals and anything that moved—especially big dogs—and I couldn't understand why. Dogs could sense my defensive mode and tense energy whenever I was around them.

One day, I went to visit a friend and met a dog that looked very similar to the one that had bitten me and taken a big chunk out of my left buttock. While sitting on the couch, pretending to be okay and staring at this dog, something unexpected happened. The dog walked straight up to me, put his big face on my lap, and looked directly into my eyes.

This was the very first time I had ever made direct eye contact with a dog. In that moment, I suddenly saw the dog as almost human, and the horrifying fear I had felt just moments earlier completely disappeared.

For the first time since I was bitten, I was sitting calmly on a couch with a big dog lying right next to me.

This was another trauma I carried with me, reactivated by a dog similar to the one that had bitten me. In that moment, that dog helped heal my trauma. Now I feel connected to everything. I see "life" in everything—yes, even in ants. **I MADE IT.**

FROM A VERY WOUNDED AND CARELESS MOTHER TO BECOMING A HAPPY AND RESPONSIBLE PARENT.

As parents, we often try to control our children to compensate for our own internal struggles, or we hold on to them too tightly or for too long, which can end up hurting or crippling both ourselves and our children.

This was the beginning of my realization as a parent. As an abused, raped, and sexually abused victim, I became an overly protective mother to my oldest daughter, trying to shield her from any of her male friends. It took time for me to recognize that I was reacting and parenting my daughter based on my own trauma.

I realized that I had been dragging my oldest daughter into the life I had unconsciously created, trying to comfort my own pain and fill my internal voids.

After years of struggling and feeling helpless as a single parent, I realized that I needed to parent myself first—get healthy as a parent in order to properly raise my children and help them grow into healthy individuals.

The first major decision I made was to tell my oldest daughter, the moment she turned eighteen, that she was free to go and discover her own life lessons after years of rebelling.

Today, more than a decade later, she has grown into a fully independent woman, a wonderful mother, and an even better parent than I was when I started.

As the American poet, memoirist, and civil rights activist
Maya Angelou said:
"I did then what I knew how to do; now that I know
better, I do better."

Another profound experience I had in my healing journey was recognizing that every experience has its own threshold—a point where you reach your maximum tolerance. When you reach that point, it can either make you snap and act out destructively, or make you quit, surrender completely, and become free.

And because my desire to feel better was stronger than anything, that part of me automatically chose the path of letting go and surrendering. Each time I reached that point—whether it was anger, frustration, irritation, or excitement—I let go and surrendered.

After more than a decade of enduring constant battles, harassment, and disrespect from the father of my older children, one day I snapped and said, "Enough is enough." Every part of me was ready to let go, and I surrendered completely. I gave up the battle and chose peace—for all of us.

I quietly, peacefully, and deliberately detached, giving my children the freedom to decide for themselves whatever makes them happy—even if that meant never seeing me again. It freed me completely.

Having been a severely abused child, I live by the conviction I gained from years of agonizing experiences: no innocent child deserves to be punished for something they did not consciously or willingly create or ask for themselves.

When your own inner peace, happiness, and well-being become the most important and valuable things to you, you naturally let go of everything that no longer serves you. You also learn to protect the innocents and those who can't fight for themselves.

It can mean making sacrifices by honoring the wishes of those you deeply love and care about—even if it goes against your own will. That difficult decision taught me the profound and deeper meaning of parenting.

You win the war by giving up the battle—with courage and dignity—to create peace for everyone." The rest automatically falls into place once you learn to trust and follow your truths.

Raising my youngest daughter while healing as a parent completely transformed the way I parented. By this time, I had already met my younger self and returned to that childlike state of being.

My youngest daughter became my mission, and I vowed to myself that she would never grow up in an unhappy, unhealthy, destructive, or abusive environment.

I made sure to create that environment for her. And that healthy, happy environment begins with being a healthy and happy parent. No unfair rules, no harsh discipline—just being a joyful, rational, healthy, and carefree mother for my daughter to witness.

Soon I began to realize that we don't raise our children through strict rules, harsh discipline, commands, or demands—whether for homework, chores, or controlling every action. We raise them by being role models, demonstrating through our own behavior the kind of person we want them to become.

We raise our children by example—by how we behave, how we speak, how we eat, the clothes we wear, the words we use when communicating with them, and how we treat others in their presence. This is how children learn, and this is how we raise healthy, happy, and strong children.

Applying this approach with my youngest daughter and observing how she is growing, I realized there is no better way to raise children than by modeling the behavior we want them to adopt as adults.

Children mimic us; they absorb much of what we do and how we act around them. They develop traits, character, and even aspects of their personality from the example we set, and their self-confidence and self-image grow from the confidence and self-image we demonstrate in front of them.

We mold our children into the adults they will become by how we are around them. I am now a New-Born Parent. I may not have had the best role models growing up, but how my parents raised me taught me some of the biggest lessons any parent could receive.

I became the parent I wanted for myself and for my children. Coming from a place of deep wounds, not knowing how to love properly—or even what "love" truly felt like—healing myself gave me all the answers.

Healing gave me the infinite capacity to love and forgive. I MADE IT. Love is the answer to all pain.

FROM THE SEVERELY ABUSED VICTIM AND HELPLESS CODEPENDENT TO BECOMING A SURVIVOR AND A THRIVER.

As part of my healing process and revisiting past life events, I reconnected with the narcissistic person four years after the divorce—this time with my eyes wide open.

I wanted to witness how everything had truly unfolded. It was a remarkable experience to see past events being recreated in real time—while I was fully awake, aware, and consciously experiencing everything. After a few weeks of close interaction with this person, I recognized that his behavior no longer resonated with me.

I noticed myself feeling completely present and grounded in awareness, consciously observing him act from a place of unconsciousness. That was the moment I found closure and resolution for everything that had remained unresolved. I was no longer seeing him through the lens of my past pain. I was seeing him exactly as he was.

In that moment, my false narrative about him dissolved, and I finally perceived him clearly and truthfully.

One day, I had another profoundly intense out-of-body experience with the same person, watching myself being triangulated with two other women. I suddenly became conscious and fully aware of what was happening.

I was speechless, witnessing the simultaneous shift within me—from being asleep to becoming fully awake and realizing the truth of the situation.

Another time, I was on the phone with him when he began calling me names, triggering memories of the way he used to speak to me in the past. In that moment, I noticed how calm I was. I did not react at all.

My emotional attachment to him lifted out of me, as if something had been pulled directly from my chest. The familiar feeling of being verbally abused became nothing more than a fleeting wave of negative energy that passed through me for a split second—and then disappeared.

I felt no emotional reaction. The narcissistic abuse trauma finally released from my body and became simply memories of the past. **I MADE IT THROUGH.**

As I was finishing the final edit of this book, I encountered yet another narcissist—specifically, a sadistic narcissist. This person was the most unconscious, destructive, out-of-control, and high-conflict individual I had ever met.

He deliberately and aggressively targeted people through gaslighting, emotional abuse, and manipulation to get what he wanted.

This time, I immediately recognized the familiar behaviors, triggered by memories of my past experiences with narcissistic individuals.

The moment I became aware of his recognizable patterns and character traits, I distanced myself. Yet, for some reason, something within me still felt drawn back to him, even after repeated negative experiences.

Instead of resisting that powerful impulse, I acknowledged it—almost as if a force of nature was pushing me in that direction. However, this time I stayed vigilant and protective of myself while cautiously engaging with him, observing the brief moments of kindness and apparent stability he displayed.

The destructive dance continued for several months, and this one was the wildest and most intense I had yet experienced in any relationship—because everything this person did was high intensity.

So much so that every time I was with him, every part of me felt drained and exhausted. He tested every personal and relationship boundary I had set for myself.

After several months of dancing and watching as this person constantly and deliberately tried to trigger me, I noticed something remarkable: I was calm. Nothing seemed to bother me.

It was in that moment that I recognized my triggers had finally left my system. The strong desire to stay with that person transformed into compassion and understanding, and I left freely and comfortably.

Life sent me this person to test my triggers, and I passed the test with flying colors. For the first time in my life, I honored my truths, stood up for myself, lived up to my personal and moral standards, and chose myself. I walked out and said goodbye to this person peacefully.

You always know if you've made the right decision because every part of you agrees with it. **I MADE IT THROUGH.**

FROM A SEVERE PEOPLE-PLEASER, HELPLESS CODEPENDENT, AND DEPENDENT WOMAN TO BECOMING FULLY INDEPENDENT, SELF-SUFFICIENT, AND SELF-RELIANT

The woman who once believed she could never survive without someone to depend on, please, or save—I am now internally strong enough to never again try to change, save, or fix anyone—or try to solve everyone's problems, and I no longer allow anyone to "save" me from my own.

I have learned to let go of anyone who doesn't serve me in any way. I let them walk their own path and learn from their choices and mistakes, while I continue to walk my own path peacefully.

Healing myself made me understand the true meaning of life and taught me how to live fully and unconditionally. Now, I wake up every day feeling whole, happy, healthy, and complete—needing no one.

I realized that I had become the woman I never knew I could become. A romantic relationship is no longer a necessity but a matter of choice. **I MADE IT.**

FROM BROKEN RELIGIOUS PRACTICE TO FINDING MY TRUE FAITH

I grew up practicing a very strict, cult-like religion, with countless moral codes to follow—while the preachers and teachers often did the exact opposite of what they preached. This led me to develop very confused beliefs about what and who "God" really was.

Later, being married to someone who believed in nothing and constantly mocked me for my faith completely shook my foundation. I lost my footing entirely—unsure of what or whom to believe.

The one thing I had embodied since I was a little girl, though, was the ability to sit in quiet places whenever I was hurt—deeply feeling and sensing everything. Over time, I lost this connection.

It wasn't until my weakest moments, battling severe depression, that I was reminded of it. Remembering how to pray during that journey is when I discovered the True Nature of God.

The God I knew was always there, but I could never quite grasp it whenever I tried to reach out—until one day, I woke up and suddenly recognized that I finally understood. It showed up for me when I needed it most—I was ready and I was willing to listen, and so I heard—loud and clear.

However you choose to call your inner strength, I found mine in the darkest hours of my life, and it helped me get through. I found "**LIFE**", the meaning of life, and my deep connection to it.

I found God—and my own understanding of religion. A faith shaped by my personal understanding of God and how to apply it in everything I do.

God exists in each of us—in everything we do, everywhere we go. You need to find your own connection in a way that feels right and true to you, regardless of the religion, spiritual path, or practice you choose.

That is all that truly matters—and no one else needs to know. Live in that truth and conviction.

Living a life with a wide-open heart and mind about God, I can resonate with every human being, regardless of the faith or religious beliefs they practice. I know that we are all one and the same—we all want to live in the harmony of love.

We all desire a life that feels true to us: relationships that feel right, a job we love, friends who inspire and uplift us, family that supports us and keeps us grounded, and raising healthy and happy children.

We all want to wake up every day feeling good, knowing that we are creating and living a life that feels authentic to us—regardless of how others live theirs. What matters is that we are living in our truths, because truth sets us free. I made it through my darkest journey.

So, what is depression? Depression is the manifestation—the symptoms, or the surface reactions—of years or decades of suppressed, unconscious, and unresolved emotional and psychological trauma. The moment you become aware of them, your healing begins.

I lived in deep pain and suffering for the first thirty-nine years of my life. I reached a point where I was psychologically drained and physically exhausted, living in a state of depression, unhappiness, and misery. I didn't know any other way to live or experience life because that was all I had ever known.

It was only when I became aware of my unconscious traumas and surrendered to the agony of the healing process that I began to recognize there was another way to live and experience life.

Now, I am experiencing life beyond what I once believed possible—so real and so profound that it's difficult to fully comprehend what it feels like to be internally whole and healthy.

The **Greek philosopher Aristotle** said:
"Knowing yourself is the beginning of all wisdom."

The magnitude of the journey of healing and self-discovery is a path every human being should take. Only through this journey can one truly experience what it feels like to be fully human—and come to understand the meaning of life.

Healing and self-discovery allowed me to see, understand, and experience all facets of life and what it truly means to be human. It was the most excruciating, complex, and terrifying journey—but also the most exciting, thrilling, fulfilling, empowering, and rewarding one anyone can take.

The impact of my powerful panic attack was the moment I awakened. It was the first time I had ever experienced something so profound within myself. It led me to seek its meaning and marked the beginning of my life's journey to discover the purpose and reason I was born.

In the darkest part of my healing journey, I found the deepest part of myself—which I now call **"THE SOUL."** That deepest part of us is always waiting to be found and freed.

When I reached this stage of my healing, I knew the long road of my suffering had finally come to an end—because it felt like there was nowhere else to go.

I HAVE ARRIVED.

I AM FINALLY HOME.

Hello, my dearest readers,

Thank You for taking this journey with me.

My name is **Alexandra Zane Royale,**

and I will see you on the other side.

— THE END AND THE NEW BEGINNING —

THE AUTHOR

Alexandra Z. Royale

Website: www.alexandraroyale.com

Social Media: Alexandra Z. Royale

(Facebook, X, Instagram, Thread, YouTube)

Other Books Available

FEELINGS ENCYCLOPEDIA: Understand Your Feelings

100 MOST COMMON FEELINGS: A Quick and Healthy Guide to Manage Your Feelings

FEELINGS: You Can't Control What You Don't Know. Recognize It. Name It. Experience It. Learn from It.